More Mastery

MORE
Mastery

VOCABULARY FOR
ACADEMIC READING

Linda Wells *and* Gladys Valcourt
College of Education, Temple University

Ann Arbor

THE UNIVERSITY OF MICHIGAN PRESS

For Lyle and Mary Vogel
with love and thanks

Acknowledgments

This book would not have come into print without the continuing enthusiasm and guidance of our editor, Kelly Sippell, and the staff at the University of Michigan Press; the artistic talent of Mary Fore; ideas, advice, and feedback from our colleagues and students; and the unlimited patience and support of our families. To all, our very sincere thanks.

The authors and publishers would like to thank the following for permission to reproduce copyrighted material in this text. Every effort has been made to identify all copyrighted material and obtain permission for its use.

Unit 1
Excerpts from *Billie Jean* by Billie Jean King. Copyright © 1974 by Billie Jean King. Reprinted by permission of HarperCollins Publishers, Inc.

Unit 2
Excerpts from *Life and Death in Shanghai* by Nien Cheng. Copyright © 1986 by Nien Cheng. Used by permission of Grove/Atlantic, Inc.

Unit 3
Excerpts from *Into Thin Air* by Jon Krakauer. Copyright © 1997 by Jon Krakauer. Reprinted by permission of Villard Books, a division of Random House, Inc.

Unit 4
Excerpts from *Personal History* by Katharine Graham. Copyright © 1997 by Katharine Graham. Reprinted by permission of Alfred A. Knopf, Inc.

Unit 5
From *The Living Tradition of María Martínez* by Susan Peterson. Copyright © 1977 by Kodansha International. Reprinted by permission. All rights reserved.

Unit 6
Reprinted with the permission of Scribner, a Division of Simon & Schuster from *Seasons of Her Life* by Ann Blackman. Copyright © 1998 by Ann Blackman.

Unit 7
Excerpts from *Ansel Adams: A Biography* by Mary Street Alinder, copyright © 1996 by Mary Street Alinder. Reprinted by permission of Henry Holt and

Company, LLC, and the Miriam Altshuler Literary Agency on behalf of Mary Street Alinder.

Photograph of Ansel Adams © James Alinder.

Unit 8
Excerpts from *Thurgood Marshall: American Revolutionary* by Juan Williams. Copyright © 1998 by Juan Williams. Reprinted by permission of Times Books, a division of Random House, Inc.

Unit 9
Excerpts adapted from *Many Masks: A Life of Frank Lloyd Wright* by Brendan Gill. Putnam, 1987.

Photograph of the Imperial Hotel courtesy of The Frank Lloyd Wright Archives, Scottsdale, AZ.

Photograph of Fallingwater by Robert P. Ruschak courtesy of the Western Pennsylvania Conservancy.

All portraits of the subjects used by permission of the artist, Mary Fore. Copyright © 1999.

Contents

Contents / xi

Introduction

More Mastery, an academic reader built around the achievements of renowned Americans, introduces English as a second language students to the University Word List (UWL). The approximately 800 high-frequency words on this list, developed by Xue Guoyi and Paul Nation in 1984, are the English words most widely used in academic settings, that is, those that occur frequently across many disciplines. Adding the words from this list to a basic English vocabulary of 2,000 words will enable ESL learners to understand about 95 percent of the vocabulary they encounter in their academic reading.

During the writing of *More Mastery*, a new Academic Word List was developed by Averil Coxhead (1998). This new list contains approximately 575 words that occur frequently in written academic English. There is a great deal of overlap between the Academic Word List (1998) and the University Word List (1984), with only 183 of the words on the new Academic Word List not appearing on the University Word List. We would suggest that students add these 183 words to the 800-word University Word List as they continue their vocabulary study. A list of the additional 183 words is provided on pages 201–3 after the University Word List.

Theoretical Perspective

Reflecting the influence of psycholinguistic top-down approaches to reading, vocabulary instruction for the past two decades has emphasized the *implicit, incidental learning of words*. The focus has been on directing students to use the least number of cues to arrive at meaning and to infer from context whenever possible. New research findings suggest, however, that combining this top-down approach with strong *explicit, bottom-up skills* results in increased vocabulary gains. Currently, the recommended model for vocabulary instruction is an *interactive approach* that directs students not only to infer from context but also to incorporate new words within existing schemata, experience repeated encounters with the words, engage in deeper levels of processing, and use a variety of strategies for learning and retaining words. It is this current model that serves as the theoretical framework for *More Mastery*.

More Mastery assumes that academic vocabulary is best learned when students engage in two general kinds of activities: activities aimed at using words *accurately* and activities aimed at using words *fluently.* For this reason, the units of study include both form-focused and meaning-focused vocabulary instruction. *Form-focused instruction* attends to word parts, word relationships, word origins, collocations, word meaning, and the grammar of words. *Meaning-focused instruction* attends to the communicative uses of language: listening to what a friend has to say, talking about a work of art, reading about an interesting person, or writing a report for a course.

The *listening activities* in *More Mastery* consist of listening to and working with authentic audio-taped biographical texts. Transcripts of these texts are provided in the teacher's manual. *Speaking activities* call for students to practice formulaic dialogues, engage in natural conversations, and give formal oral presentations. *Reading activities* are a key feature of the text. Reading these biographical selections provides students with a great deal of input about how the target vocabulary is commonly used in English. Additionally, the readings familiarize students with many aspects of American culture. Students read about Americans involved in business, law, social activism, sports, architecture, the arts, and many other areas of American life. This will help students to develop not only language skills but also a better understanding of American culture. A wide variety of *writing exercises,* ranging from creative writing to writing for a particular discourse community, is also included in *More Mastery*.

The theoretical framework underlying *More Mastery* emphasizes studying words separately as distinct language items and also learning them, in natural contexts, as part of a language system that is used to communicate effectively with others.

Unique Features of *More Mastery:* Critical Thinking and Cooperative Skills

In addition to the skills emphasized in the first book of the Mastery series, this second book, *More Mastery,* emphasizes critical thinking and cooperative skills. Current literature on education stresses the need for ESL students to develop the critical thinking skills required to perform successfully in the academic and work environments. Critical thinking skills are the high-level thought processes necessary for examining and weighing ideas, drawing conclusions from data, solving problems, and doing other complex abstract kinds of reasoning. Some of the critical thinking skills most needed by ESL students in their academic work are reflecting, problem solving, analysis, synthesis, and evaluation. Exercises in *More Mastery* address this need. Following the Comprehension Check at the end of each reading, the Critical Thinking section provides students with questions or tasks that have them apply critical thinking skills of this kind. In Unit 1, "Billie Jean King," for example, students are asked to analyze and evaluate. As a group, they must choose the three most important things that Billie Jean King did in order to prepare her "self" and her "game" before the tennis match against Bobby Riggs. Students must also be prepared to explain why they chose those items.

In answering the Critical Thinking questions, students are generally asked to work cooperatively within groups of three to four persons in an effort to reach their goal. Studies suggest that such a cooperative learning environment is an acquisition-rich environment for language learning. Students have to be active listeners, produce their own novel sentences, negotiate for meaning, and maintain coherence at a discourse level, all of which facilitate acquisition. In *More Mastery* the development of cooperative skills occurs not only in the Critical Thinking section but also throughout the Word Study exercises, particularly in the communicative listening and speaking exercises.

Organization

More Mastery consists of twelve units. Nine of the units introduce new vocabulary in readings about 1,500 words long; three review units recycle words already studied. The units are presented according to graded levels of reading difficulty, with earlier units being easier than later ones.

More Mastery is a user-friendly text that contains a number of features to facilitate student learning and teacher instruction. These include glossed words and phrases, easily scored review tests, and three appendixes: the University Word List, the Answer Key, and instructions on how to make vocabulary index cards and a vocabulary notebook.

Suggestions for the Self-Study Student

More Mastery can be used for self-study by learners who are not enrolled in an ESL program but who want to improve their vocabulary on their own. If you are one of these learners, here are some suggestions for using the text.

1. Find out how much you already know by completing the Vocabulary Preview (at the beginning of each unit) and the Review sections of the text.
2. Go over the list of words in the Word Study section of the unit and cross out those that you already know.
3. Locate the remaining words in the reading passage and see if, from the context, you can guess what the words mean.
4. Consult your dictionary for the meanings of words you do not know. Write these in a vocabulary notebook. By the time you finish the notebook, you will have your own academic learner dictionary.
5. Work your way through the Vocabulary Preview and the reading selections of the unit. Check your dictionary for words not listed on your vocabulary list that are essential to your understanding of the reading.
6. As you read, check for comprehension by asking yourself periodically: Did I understand what I just read? Which sentence is giving me a problem? Why? What or who can help me understand this?
7. Also, as you are reading, stop to predict what is coming next. Is the reading passage going to give more details about an idea already presented? Is a new idea going to be presented?
8. Following the Comprehension Check, which checks on how well you have understood the literal meaning of the reading, *More Mastery* asks questions aimed at developing your *critical thinking* skills. These are the skills used in understanding and evaluating information. After

the Unit 2 "Nien Cheng" readings, for example, the Comprehension Check asks you to say whether or not this item is correct: *Nien Cheng was confined in a detention house for more than six years.* This task requires low-level thinking skills because the answer is a simple *Yes* or *No.* But look at one of the critical thinking skills questions in this unit: *How did communism and Mao's policies affect human relationships?* Here the thinking is different because it is more complex. Here you have to start by clarifying the issue (*Did communism and Mao's policies affect human relationships?*); then you have to come up with a conclusion (*Yes, they did; No, they didn't*). Your conclusion, however, must be based on solid evidence. So you have to engage in a process of analysis: What information is there in the text to support my conclusion? What other information do I have to support my answer? Where can I get additional information about the topic? Analyzing, evaluating, obtaining the right facts—these are the high-level skills involved in making judgments. In your academic work, you will be expected to think critically, to reach rational conclusions, and to make responsible choices, rather than accept whatever information comes your way. The Critical Thinking questions at the end of each unit of *More Mastery* will help you develop these skills.

9. Find a friend or a tutor who can help you with the communicative activities—someone who will listen to you and talk with you. Literacy councils and local libraries have volunteer tutors who can help. Or, check with the international student center in your university. These centers often have tutors to help ESL students with their English.

10. Scan the Word Study section of the unit and complete those activities that you think might help you learn. Skip those that seem too easy for you. The listening exercises, as well as the vocabulary words and one or more of the readings from each unit, are on the *More Mastery* audiotape. They are marked with this symbol 🎧.

11. When you have finished all of the activities you selected, turn to the Answer Key and check your answers.

12. Reread the reading selection to find out if the reading has become much easier to understand.

13. Use supplementary materials such as books, magazine articles, and videos to expand your knowledge of the topic. The web page for

Biography on the Internet (http://www.biography.com), for example, advertises videos for Madeleine Albright, Thurgood Marshall, and Frank Lloyd Wright.

Working your way through *More Mastery* will help you to master the words needed for successful academic achievement. It will also enrich your understanding of the people and culture of the United States. We wish you success in your studies!

Richland Center, Wisconsin
San Ildefonso, New Mexico
Topeka, Kansas
Bear Run, Pennsylvania
Washington, DC
Long Beach, California
Hernandez, New Mexico
Prague, Czech Republic
Mt. Everest
Tokyo, Japan
Shanghai, China

Locations referred to in readings

Unit 1
Billie Jean King

Vocabulary Preview

Preview 1

The following sentences contain information that appears in the reading on Billie Jean King. Complete each one with the most suitable word.

accuracy   atmosphere   injury   rhythm   stressful

1. When Billie Jean practiced with Pete Collins she tried to concentrate on

   each shot and on getting a good _____ going.

2. Hitting different types of serves is difficult. It takes _____ and precision to do it consistently.

3. Before a match, Billie Jean always liked to walk around the court to

   feel the _____ of the place where she would play.

4. Just before the match against Bobby Riggs, Billie Jean worried about losing—not just for herself but for all women in tennis. It was one of

   the most _____ hours of her life.

5. At the rules meeting before the match the players decided to have a

   special ten-minute _____ time-out.

Preview 2

Look at the way the underlined words are used in the sentences. Match each word with its definition.

1. A special material on the outside of the space shuttle absorbs heat and prevents the shuttle from burning up as it reenters the earth's atmosphere.

2. The flight from London is scheduled to arrive in New York at approximately 9:30 P.M.

3. The doctor assured the couple that their child would recover within a few days.

4. It is risky to order goods through the Internet with a credit card, unless you are using a secure on-line server.

5. In the late 1950s, consumer taste <u>shifted</u> away from economy cars, and people began to buy sporty, more luxurious cars.

__ 1. absorbs	a. safe
__ 2. approximately	b. moved; changed
__ 3. assured	c. soaks up; takes in
__ 4. secure	d promised
__ 5. shifted	e. about; around

Reading Preview: What Do You Know about Billie Jean King?

Circle the correct answer. If you don't know the answer, guess.

1. Billie Jean King is
   a. a famous Olympic gymnast
   b. a popular television sports reporter
   c. the daughter of Martin Luther King, Jr.
   d. one of the greatest female tennis players of all time

2. Which of these sports tournaments did Billie Jean King *not* win?
   a. Wimbledon
   b. the American Open
   c. the World Series
   d. the Australian Open

3. The tennis match between Billie Jean King and Bobby Riggs became a symbol of
   a. the women's movement
   b. the Civil Rights movement
   c. the gay pride movement
   d. the antiwar movement

Adapted from *Billie Jean* by Billie Jean King with Kim Chapin (New York: Harper & Row, 1974), 177–86.

Introduction to the Readings

Billie Jean King was born in Long Beach, California, in 1943. As a young girl, Billie Jean was a natural athlete who showed exceptional talent in softball. Her parents, however, encouraged her to play tennis, and she quickly became a gifted player. At the age of eighteen, Billie Jean beat the world's best woman tennis player, Margaret Court Smith, at Wimbledon. During her career King went on to win Wimbledon, the French Open, the Australian Open, and the U.S. Open many times, in both singles and doubles competition.

In addition to her excellence as an athlete, Billie Jean King is known for her dedicated work to improve the treatment, and pay, of women in sports; for being the first woman athlete to earn $100,000 in a single year; and for establishing the first successful women's professional tennis tour. Billie Jean's most publicized victory may have been when she defeated Bobby Riggs in the "Battle of the Sexes" exhibition match in 1973. This "man versus woman" tennis match quickly became a symbol of the women's movement and helped to popularize the women's movement among ordinary American women. In the readings here, adapted from *Billie Jean* by Billie Jean King with Kim Chapin, Billie tells about preparing for and playing that famous match.

Reading 1: Preparing for the Match

(1)   I'd begun preparing seriously for my match against Bobby Riggs the day after I lost the match to **Chris Evert.** I got into the routine that I always try to use when I'm playing tennis at night. I forced myself to stay up late and sleep until ten or eleven in the morning. I did this so that during the match, which would take place in the evening, my body would be at its high point. I wanted to feel my very best from seven to ten o'clock at night. I did a lot of weightlifting for my legs and knees and it really helped. My legs were so strong the night of the match I couldn't believe it. I took good care of myself and got a lot of rest. And I got my head together.

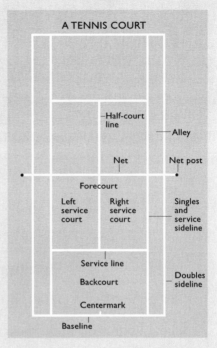

A TENNIS COURT

Half-court line
Alley
Net
Net post
Forecourt
Left service court
Right service court
Singles and service sideline
Service line
Backcourt
Doubles sideline
Centermark
Baseline

(2)   Pete Collins, the resident professional tennis instructor at **Hilton Head,** played twice a day with me for about an hour each time. We mainly just **rallied** a lot, and I tried to concentrate on each shot, each swing of the racket, to get a good rhythm going. Sometimes we just hit to see how long we could keep the ball in play, and I got very patient inside. When I get that way I can stay on the **baseline** all day if I have to.

(3)   That was going to be my alternative strategy—the baseline game. I wanted to be able to mix it up—go in some, stay back a little—. What I wanted to do at the start was to win some **volleys** because I thought that would break Bobby down faster psychologically. I also practiced a lot of volleying. I felt sure that Bobby didn't realize how quick I was or how good a volley I had. He knew, of course, I had a good volley—for a girl. But I thought my volley was strong compared to anyone, man or woman, and I was counting on him underestimating me in that respect.

Chris Evert: the young American woman who won Wimbledon in 1974
Hilton Head: The place where Billie Jean trained. This is an island resort off the coast of South Carolina.
to rally: to play a series of hits between players before a point is won
baseline: the boundary line at each end of a tennis court
volley: the process of returning or hitting the ball back before it touches the ground

(4)   I practiced shifting my service all the time, going from a hard, flat serve to a **slice** serve to a **topspin** serve to a twist. This is not easy to do with any consistency because it takes real accuracy and precision. During the match I planned to keep changing my serve around and serve the ball into his body a lot. I felt that was going to be important: to serve into him and then go wide—to make him go exceptionally wide—to always keep him off balance, because he's the type of player who relies on his own balance to keep the rally under control.

(5)   Finally, I worked on keeping my shots to his **backhand side**—his weak side—and then hitting very sharply to his **forehand.** Again, the idea was to confuse him, run him around the court, keep him from getting control, make him feel less secure.

Reading 2: Match Day

(6)   I got up around noon, had breakfast and started eating candy. I ate candy all day so that my body would have lots of energy for the match. About four in the afternoon, I went over to the **Astrodome.** It was only the second time I'd been there, and it's really important for me to get the feel of a place, the atmosphere—like I do at **Wimbledon** every year—by just walking around and absorbing a sense of where I am. I went down to the court, which was laid out approximately where second base is, and looked up and thought, "This is it. You've got to get used to this place." It was such a huge building that the feeling of space was different, not like a tennis stadium at all.

(7)   Later that afternoon I did a television interview for **ABC,** and finally went out and hit to try and get used to the court. This was the biggest problem both Bobby and I had. **This court was really dead in spots, and slow all over.** It took us both a while to adjust.

slice: a hit that does not follow a straight path
topspin: a motion that causes the ball to rotate forward in the direction it is traveling
backhand side: The side on which a backhand stroke is made. In a backhand stroke the back of the hand faces the direction of the motion of the stroke.
forehand: a stroke where the palm of the hand faces the direction of the motion of the stroke
Astrodome: a large sports stadium in Houston, Texas
Wimbledon: One of four professional tennis tournaments in the Grand Slam. This tournament takes place in England.
ABC: the name of a major U.S. television network
This court was really dead in spots, and slow all over: In some areas, the tennis ball didn't bounce very much or travel very fast. The surface of the tennis court made play slow.

(8)   After I finished hitting, I had a shower, changed clothes and had a meal before the match—then the pressure of the whole thing finally got to me. It hit me in a very strange way. I had my usual pre-match tension, of course, but beyond that, in the hour or so before the match I felt more completely alone than I ever had in my life. I just got totally wrapped up in my own thoughts. I remembered all the **hassles** and headaches of the early **Virginia Slims women's tennis tour,** and I thought about how far we women had come in such a short time. It really came home to me—hard—that if I lost to Riggs much of what we'd won for ourselves might **go right out the window.** I'd felt it before, but now I knew that this match was one of the most important in my life—a defeat would just about erase everything that I'd done before. The hour before Bobby and I actually stepped on the court was probably the most stressful one of my life.

Reading 3: The Match

(9)   Then the show began. Bobby was wheeled out onto the court in a ridiculous **rickshaw,** and I was carried out onto the court in one of those **throne-like litters.** Then Bobby presented me with a huge **Sugar Daddy lollipop**—about the size of a tennis racket—and I also gave him a gift: a little **"male chauvinist" piglet** brought in for the occasion.

(10)   When we walked out on to the court to warm up, I couldn't believe the crowd. It was really like a circus, or a baseball game, or maybe even a heavyweight title fight. Balloons, bands, noise, the works. People were shouting, "Right on, Billie Jean," or "Go, Bobby," from the moment we entered and well into the match. I loved it. Just the way a tennis crowd ought to be everywhere.

(11)   But once the match started, everything was very serious—nothing except tennis. At the rules meeting the day before, when we'd decided on things like the special ten-minute injury time-out, I'd emphasized that. I didn't

hassles: problems or difficulties
Virginia Slims women's tennis tour: a women's professional tennis tour, sponsored by the Virginia Slims cigarette company
go right out the window: a slang expression that means "be finished or over, be lost"
rickshaw: a small two-wheeled vehicle that carries passengers and is pulled by a person
throne-like litter: a fancy seat with two poles or shafts under it, that is carried by two or more people
Sugar Daddy lollipop: A type of candy on a stick. A "sugar daddy" is also a man who supports or spends a lot of money on a woman.
"male chauvinist" piglet: The derogatory term *male chauvinist pig* refers to a man who thinks he is superior to women. In this case, Billie Jean gave Bobby an actual baby pig.

want there to be any doubts at all about the match. It had to be on the level, and it was.

(12)   Just before the match began I told myself, "Okay, this is it. Take each point by itself and don't rush things." I served first and won the first game. I couldn't believe how slow Bobby was. I thought he was **faking it.** He had to be. At the change after the first game I asked my coach if Bobby was putting me on. Dennis assured me I was seeing the real thing, but I think Riggs did **coast** the first three or four games, trying to figure me out and at the same time not give away all of his wonderful secrets.

(13)   I was kind of shocked because I thought he would be a lot better than he was. He didn't have a big service, and his spins weren't that great either. And I was absolutely right about him not realizing how quick I was at the net or how well I could volley. I concentrated hard on winning that first set and when I did I knew he was in big trouble. That meant he would have to play at least four tough sets to win the match, probably more hard competitive tennis than he'd played in years. I felt I was in pretty good shape, and that things were going my way.

(14)   About halfway through the second set, I knew that the match was mine if I could just keep up the pace. But I didn't let up because I'd gotten into trouble too many times before thinking I had a match won before it was over. Everything that I thought would work before the match did work. I played conservatively those last two sets and at the end I was playing with complete confidence.

(15)   On match point I threw my racket in the air and just when I looked down I saw him finish his jump over the net. He came over to congratulate me, and then he was really nice. He said, "You're too good," and that was it. Ten weeks of **getting psyched up** for one night of tennis and then, boom, it was all over.

(16)   The match was tough, mentally and physically. I've played better matches, but under the circumstances I played as well as I possibly could, and so, I think, did Bobby. As far as the importance of the match, it proved just two things. First, that a woman can beat a man. Second, that tennis can be a **big-time sport,** and will be, once it gets into the hands of the people who know how to promote it.

Note: These excerpts were written in 1974. Tennis had not yet become the popular and lucrative sport that it is today.

faking it: pretending
to coast: to relax, to not make much effort
getting psyched up: preparing mentally for a challenge or difficult task
big-time sport: a sport that is recognized and respected as important

Comprehension Check

Check your understanding of the reading selections by marking these sentences true (*T*) or false (*F*).

___ 1. Billie Jean always got up late and went to bed late, even when she wasn't preparing for a match.
___ 2. Billie Jean wanted to break Bobby down psychologically by winning volleys at the beginning of the match.
___ 3. Bobby had a strong backhand, but his forehand was weak.
___ 4. Billie Jean ate a lot of candy before the match because she was nervous.
___ 5. Billie Jean felt that if she lost the match, it could undo all the progress that women had made in tennis.
___ 6. Billie Jean and Bobby exchanged gifts before the match.
___ 7. Billie Jean was surprised that Bobby played so slowly. She thought he was pretending.
___ 8. The match was important because it proved that men and women were equal.

Critical Thinking

These questions are designed to help you develop your *critical thinking* skills. Critical thinking skills are those used in understanding and evaluating information; the skills used to reach rational conclusions based on the information given. In order to answer these questions, you will need to engage in a process of analysis: What information is there in the text to support my conclusion? What other information do I have to support my answer? Where can I get additional information about the topic?

(For more about this section, read item 8 in "Suggestions for the Self-Study Student.")

1. Refer back to the reading and list all the things that Billie Jean did to prepare for the match with Bobby Riggs.

2. Look at your list. Which things did Billie Jean do to prepare herself for the match? Underline them. These are the "self" items. Which things were part of Billie Jean's game strategy to beat Bobby? Circle them. These are the "game" items.

3. Go back to the reading and see if you can add any more items to each category. Then compare your list with two or three other students. As a group, choose the three most important items for "self" and for "game." Be prepared to explain why you chose those items.

Word Study

 University Word List Vocabulary

absorb
accurate (accuracy)
alternative
approximate
   (approximately)
assure
atmosphere

circumstance
conserve (conservatively)
emphasize
injure (injury)
interview
physical (physically)

precise (precision)
rhythm
secure
shift
stress (stressful)
tense (tension)

Understanding Words

Word Parts

Exercise 1: Suffixes

The suffixes *-ous* and *-ive* are added to words to form adjectives. The suffix *-ous* means *full of* or *having.* For example, the word *famous* (from *fame*) means *having much fame.* The suffix *-ive* means *that which performs the indicated action.* For example, the word *exclusive* (from *exclude*) means *that which limits or excludes.* Remember, some words change spelling before adding a suffix. Check your dictionary if necessary.

A. Add either *-ous* or *-ive* to each of these words to form the words that are defined here. Write each new word on the line next to its definition.

alternate   injury   conserve   analogy   define   nerve

_____ 1. moderate or cautious; something that tends to maintain existing conditions

_____ 2. appearing to be easily excited or irritated; acting worried or frightened

_____ 3. harmful or hurtful; something that causes injury

_____ 4. something that is related to another thing or like it in a certain way

_____ 5. an option; a different choice

_____ 6. defines or specifies precisely; a perfect example of something

B. Use one of the new words to complete each of the following sentences.

1. A person who is extremely _____ may feel cold, perspire, turn pale, and tremble.

2. _____ medicine, which uses therapies like herbal medicine, massage, and acupuncture, can be just as effective as Western medicine for some illnesses.

3. "Bread" is _____ to "food," as "tea" is related to "beverage."

4. The Republican party has a _____ policy on welfare spending. The Democratic party tends to be more liberal.

5. *The Old Man and the Sea* is considered by many to be Ernest Hemingway's

_____ work.

6. Despite denial by tobacco companies, scientific research has shown

that cigarette smoking is _____ to health.

Word Relationships

Exercise 2: Synonyms

Cross out the word or phrase in each series that is not a synonym for the first word in that series. Use your dictionary if necessary.

1. approximate	estimate	exact	nearly correct
2. emphasize	ignore	stress	make prominent
3. precision	accuracy	exactness	carelessness
4. rhythm	speed	pattern	fluctuation
5. secure	dangerous	safe	guaranteed
6. stress	tension	selection	pressure

Analogies

Remember, analogies are comparisons between two sets of words.
Analogies consist of four words, three of which are always given.
The analogy is completed by adding a fourth word to complete the
connection.

Example:
A waiter is to a restaurant as a teller is to a bank.
waiter : restaurant :: teller : ___bank_____

A doctor is to the body as a dentist is to teeth.
doctor : body :: dentist : _____

Exercise 3: Analogies

Use one of the words from the word lists in Units 1, 2, or 3 to complete
the analogy. Change the word form by adding a word ending if necessary.
Use your dictionary if you are unsure of a word's meaning.

1. solid : earth :: gas : _____

2. mind : mental :: body : _____

3. give off : secrete :: take in : _____

4. unique : distinct :: different : _____

5. square : cube :: circle : _____

6. cover : expose :: lower : _____

Word Meanings and Forms

Read the definitions for the word *shift* given here.

A. *shift* v: 1. to change place, position, or direction; 2. to change gears
B. *shift* n: 1. a loose-fitting or semifitted dress; 2. a shirt
C. *shift* n: a scheduled period of work or other duty

Exercise 4: Multiple Meanings of *Shift*

Look at the way the word *shift* is used in the following sentences and then write the letter of the meaning that best fits *shift* in each sentence. If the definition is divided into numbered parts (as in definitions A and B), also include the part number. Why did you choose that meaning? Write your reason on the line given.

_____ 1. While driving, be sure to push in the clutch before attempting to shift gears.

　　　　 Reason: _____

_____ 2. Many factory workers prefer to work either the day or evening shift, rather than the night shift, even though the night shift pays higher wages.

　　　　 Reason: _____

_____ 3. Billie Jean shifted her weight from side to side as she waited for Bobby to serve.

　　　　 Reason: _____

_____ 4. The weather was very hot, so the girl wore a light shift and sandals.

　　　　 Reason: _____

_____ 5. If you shift the books around, you can probably fit a couple more in the box.

　　　　 Reason: _____

Exercise 5: Word Forms

Complete each sentence with the correct word.

1. The television _____ asked the president several tough questions about the new foreign policy.
   interview　　interviewer　　interviewee　　interviewed

2. Billie Jean was _____ about allowing a ten-minute injury time-out.
   emphasis　　emphasizes　　emphatic　　emphasized

3. The new paper towels are more _____, so consumers will actually save money by using fewer of them.

   absorb   absorbent   absorption   absorbed

4. The man looked young; I'd say he was _____ twenty years old.

   approximate   approximately   approximated   approximation

5. The express train is always on time; it arrives at _____ 5:02.

   precise   precision   precisely   imprecise

Understanding Words in Sentences

Exercise 6: Word Meanings in Context

In the reading passages, scan for the words given in the following list. The number of the paragraph containing the word is given in parentheses. Circle the letter of the meaning that is most appropriate within the context of the reading passage.

1. rhythm (2)
   a. pace or speed
   b. natural flow of movement
   c. a beat

2. accuracy (4)
   a. exactness
   b. concentration
   c. energy

3. tension (8)
   a. force
   b. hostility
   c. the opposite of relaxation

4. emphasized (11)
   a. neglected
   b. stressed
   c. wondered about

5. assured (12)
   a. gave
   b. believed
   c. guaranteed

6. circumstances (16)
   a. situation or conditions
   b. evidence
   c. facts

Exercise 7: Word Meanings in Context

Find the words in the reading passages that have the following meanings and write these words on the lines provided. Change the word form by adding or deleting a word ending if necessary. The number in parentheses is the number of the paragraph where the word occurs.

1. one of two or more choices (3) _____

2. change from one to another (4) _____

3. the mood or feeling of a place (6) _____

4. a meeting where information is obtained (7) _____

5. cautiously; not taking risks (14) _____

6. having to do with the body (16) _____

Exercise 8: Constructing Sentences

Use each set of words to write a question. (No additional words are needed.)

1. was / at / Billie Jean's / she / routine / night? / when / played / What / tennis

_____

2. alternative / was / strategy? / Billie Jean's / What / game

_____

3. are / and / precision / needed / tennis? / Why / in / accuracy

_____

4. hour / Billie Jean? / was / the / Why / before / for / match / so / the / stressful

_____

5. ten-minute / Who / injury / the / emphasized / time-out?

_____

6. physically / Do / harder / think / the / was / or / match / mentally? / you

_____

Using Words in Communication

 ### Exercise 9: Listening

Listen to the sentences on the audiotape. Then listen again and try to fill in the missing words or phrases. When you are finished, compare your answers to those given in the Answer Key.

1. I was _____ _____ _____ because I thought he would be a lot better than he was. He didn't have a big service, and his spins _____ _____ _____ either.

2. And I was _____ _____ about him not _____ how quick I was at the net or how well I could volley.

3. I _____ _____ on winning that first set and when I did I knew he was in big trouble. That meant he would have to play

   _____ _____ four tough sets to win the match,

   probably more hard _____ tennis than he'd played in years.

4. I felt I was in pretty _____ _____, and that things

   were going _____ way.

Exercise 10: Reading

Women have become top athletes in track and field, gymnastics, figure skating, tennis, golf, and basketball. Choose a female athlete who interests you and then go to the library to find information about her. Consult recent encyclopedia yearbooks, the library catalogs, and periodicals or ask the reference librarian to help you locate information. You may also want to look on the Internet by using a web browser like "Yahoo." Be prepared to give a three- to five-minute presentation about the person you choose.

Exercise 11: Speaking

Use the following questions to interview another student about the athlete he or she researched for Exercise 10.

1. Who is the person?

2. Where is she from?

3. What sport is she most known for?

4. Is she an amateur or a professional athlete? If professional, when did she become a professional?

5. Has she set any records or won any important competitions in this sport?

6. How old was she when she started participating in this sport?

7. Why did you choose this person?

Exercise 12: Writing

Discuss these questions with several classmates. Then write a short essay (three or four paragraphs) based on your discussion.

1. Was the match between Billie Jean King and Bobby Riggs important? Why or why not?
2. What, if anything, did Billie Jean's victory over Bobby Riggs prove? Was anything changed by this match?
3. Do you feel men and women should be able to compete against each other in sports? Why or why not?

Unit 2
Nien Cheng

Vocabulary Preview

Preview 1

Complete each sentence with the most suitable word.

assets   confined   episode   inhibited   policy

1. Relationships were _____ when people could not speak openly to one another.

2. The strange _____ concerning Nien's brother and the photo of the Sun Yatsen Memorial shows how political pressure made family members speak out against each other.

3. The prisoner was _____ in a "detention house" for more than six years before she found out that her daughter was dead.

4. The government took all of her _____, including her home, personal belongings, and money, when she was put into prison.

5. Mao's _____ was to find and destroy the members of other political parties, especially members of the Kuomintang.

Preview 2

Look at the way the underlined words are used in the sentences. Match each word with its definition.

1. The <u>cell</u> was a small unheated room with a dirt floor; it contained a bench for sleeping on, one tiny window, and a bucket of water.
2. People were forced to inform on one another, which had a very <u>detrimental</u> effect on relationships.
3. <u>Intense</u> pressure caused even educated and intelligent people to break down and speak out against their friends and family members.
4. It was <u>obvious</u> that she would need warm clothes to survive another winter in the unheated prison.
5. Then something strange <u>occurred;</u> a large bundle of clothing was brought to her cell by a guard.

___ 1. cell
___ 2. detrimental
___ 3. intense
___ 4. obvious
___ 5. occurred

a. causing physical or emotional injury
b. happened
c. evident; clear to see
d. a small room, often in a prison
e. strong; powerful

Reading Preview: What Do You Know about Nien Cheng and China?

Circle the correct answer. If you don't know the answer, guess.

1. Nien Cheng was
    a. a political prisoner in China for nearly seven years
    b. the wife of Mao Zedong
    c. a leader of the pro-democracy movement in China
    d. a poor, uneducated peasant woman

2. Until the early twentieth century, China was ruled by
    a. a communist form of government
    b. an imperial family
    c. a democratic form of government
    d. a parliamentary form of government

3. Mao Zedong was
    a. a member of the Chinese imperial family
    b. killed during the Tiananmen Square demonstrations in 1989
    c. one of the founders of the Chinese Communist Party
    d. born into a very wealthy family

Adapted from *Life and Death in Shanghai* by Nien Cheng (New York: Grove Press, 1986), 285–86, 339–44.

Introduction to the Readings

In her book *Life and Death in Shanghai* Nien Cheng writes with great honesty and courage about the difficult years she spent as a political prisoner during China's **Cultural Revolution.** Nien Cheng was born in **Beijing,** China, in 1915. In the 1930s she studied at the London School of Economics, where she met her husband, who was also a student. The two returned to China, married, and had a daughter, Meiping. From 1939 to 1949 Cheng's husband worked as a diplomat for the **Kuomintang** government offices in Shanghai. He left his government job in 1950 and became the general manager of the Shanghai office of Shell International Petroleum Company. After her husband's death in 1957, Cheng went to work for Shell as an assistant and adviser to the new British general manager.

During the time of Mao's Cultural Revolution, anyone with wealth, education, or connections to foreign groups was suspected of being an enemy of the communist state. Nien Cheng's connections to a foreign oil company and the Kuomintang government resulted in her arrest in 1966. She was fifty-one years old. She was imprisoned as a suspected spy for nearly seven years. During that time she was never tried for or convicted of any crime. After her release from prison in 1973, Cheng continued to live in Shanghai. She left China and immigrated to the United States in 1980.

In the first reading here, Cheng gives a very personal account of the terrible effects that the communist government's policies had on personal relationships. In the second reading, Cheng tells how, during her time in prison, she found out about the death of her daughter, Meiping, which had occurred six years earlier.

Cultural Revolution: The period from 1966 until 1976, during which Mao attempted to destroy traditional Chinese culture, and anything that was capitalist or antisocialist, in order to promote his communist ideals. Much of this destruction was carried out by the "Red Guards"—militant groups of school-aged young people.
Beijing: The capital city of the People's Republic of China. Beijing is in the northeastern part of China and was previously referred to as "Peking."
Kuomintang: The name of the Nationalist political party that established the Nationalist Republic of China in Taiwan after Mao and the communists came to power in mainland China in 1949. The Kuomintang party, led by Chiang Kai-shek, was opposed to communism.

Reading 1: "Confess!"

(1)   One of the ugliest aspects of life in China during the time of **Mao Zedong** was the **Communist Party**'s demand that people inform on one another and speak out against each other. This had a detrimental effect on human relationships. Husbands and wives did not speak openly to each other, and parents could not trust their children. It inhibited all forms of human contact, so that people no longer wanted to have friends. It also encouraged secrets and lies. In order to protect themselves, people kept their thoughts to themselves. When forced to speak, people often lied in order to protect themselves and their family.

(2)   While I was being pressured to provide information which could be used against other people, those people were being pressured to provide information that could be used against me. I could usually guess what my relatives and friends had written about me from the questions I was being asked. It was not difficult to discern whether a certain relative or friend was still calm and in control or whether he had become frightened and confused. Towards the end of 1969, I went through a difficult episode because of a "confession" made by my brother in Beijing. It is a good example of how a perfectly intelligent and educated person could **break down** under intense pressure and become unable to separate fact from fiction.

(3)   Mao had made another speech. He had declared, "The Cultural Revolution is a political revolution of the **working class** against the **capitalist class.**

Mao Zedong: the man who founded the communist People's Republic of China in 1949 and was the leader of that country until his death in 1976
Communist Party: The political party of Mao Zedong. Communism was originally based on the theories of Karl Marx and Vladimir Lenin, which proposed the elimination of social classes and private property and the equal distribution of goods and property to all members of society. Mao developed a unique type of communism in China.
to break down: to physically or mentally collapse or fall apart
working class: the class of people who work for wages
capitalist class: the class of people who have accumulated goods and property; the wealthy

It is also a part of the struggle by the Communist Party against the Kuomintang." After the publication of this speech, an effort was made to find any remaining members of the Kuomintang. The atmosphere became very tense. The speech provided an excuse for more **witch-hunts** and created fear in the general public. The only way for people to prove their loyalty was to show exaggerated support for Mao and the Party, to shout Mao's words louder and to be extra cruel to the "class enemies."

(4)   The next call for my questioning did not surprise me. My **interrogator** had to discuss "class struggle" and my connections to the Kuomintang with me if he wanted to appear to be following Mao's policies. After all, I was the **widow** of a Kuomintang government official.

(5)   I entered the room where I was to be questioned and bowed to the picture of Mao. The interrogator said, "We are to expose the last members of the Kuomintang. You are one of them."

Two men from Beijing were in the room. Suddenly the younger of them shouted, "Confess!"

"To what?" I asked.

"Don't pretend to be calm and innocent. Confess your relationship with the Kuomintang!"

"I have no relationship with the Kuomintang."

"You are a loyal member of the Kuomintang. It's useless to deny it."

"Please prove what you are saying," I said.

"Have you ever had your photograph taken in front of a Kuomintang flag?" asked my interrogator.

"Maybe I have. I can't remember for sure," I answered.

"Think back to 1962. What happened in 1962?"

"I don't know what happened in 1962, except that was the year I lost my mother."'

"That's right!" declared both men from Beijing. "You had better confess and tell the whole story."

"Do you mean you want to hear about my mother's death?" I was surprised and puzzled. I had no idea what they were trying to find out. But since they wanted to know, I told them about my mother's death.

"What did you do after your mother's death?"

---

witch-hunt: the searching out and persecution of persons with unpopular views or ideas
interrogator: a person who systematically questions someone, often a police officer or a military or legal investigator
widow: a woman whose husband has died

"Being the oldest child, I arranged her funeral. My mother was a devout **Buddhist,** so I arranged for her to have a Buddhist funeral."

"And tell me, what did you do after your mother's funeral? After you left the cemetery, where did you go?" All three of the men now seemed to become excited.

"Nowhere. We returned to her house directly."

"Didn't you go to the **Sun Yatsen Memorial** after your mother's funeral?" asked the older man from Beijing.

"No, we were all so sad and exhausted."

"Confess!" The young man suddenly pounded on the table.

"What do you want me to confess? The funeral of my mother has no political significance."

"No, but your going to the Sun Yatsen Memorial with your brothers to have your photograph taken in front of a Kuomintang flag had a great deal of political significance. You wanted to promise your loyalty to the Kuomintang. At that time, in 1962, the Kuomintang was planning to attack mainland China," said the young man.

(6)   This idea was so crazy that I wanted to laugh. But I knew the situation was actually very serious. "Please be reasonable. Assuming that you are correct in saying that I wanted to impress the Kuomintang in case they came back to the mainland, would the Kuomintang accept my declaration of loyalty simply because I could show them such a photograph? The Kuomintang officials are not fools. Wouldn't they become extremely suspicious of my motives, since they knew that my late husband and I chose to remain here in 1949 and did not follow them back to **Taiwan**?"

"They would believe you. You are already an agent for the Kuomintang," the young man yelled.

Both the men from Beijing shouted, "You must confess that you did have a photograph taken with your brothers in front of a Kuomintang flag at the Sun Yatsen Memorial in **Nanjing.**"

"Please ask my brothers and sisters-in-law. They'll tell you it did not happen. We never went to the Sun Yatsen Memorial in Nanjing at all."

"We did ask your brother at the Foreign Trade Institute in Beijing. At first

Buddhist: a person who believes in the religion of Buddhism
Sun Yatsen Memorial: a memorial in Nanjing, China, built to honor the Chinese statesman Sun Yatsen (1866–1925)
Taiwan: an island off of the southeast coast of China, which became what is still the noncommunist Nationalist Republic of China in 1949
Nanjing: a city in eastern China

he also tried to deny everything. But when the **Revolutionaries** made him see the right path to take, he confessed everything. He said it was your idea to go to the Sun Yatsen Memorial. He also said it was your camera that was used to take the photograph. You had the film developed in Shanghai and sent him a copy of it. Do you still dare to deny it?" the young man shouted.

(7)   My heart sank. It was all untrue of course, an elaborate lie. What had the Maoists done to my poor brother to make him lie like that? I could imagine the pain he went through before he collapsed under their pressure.

Reading 2: Winter Clothes

(8)   Winter was again approaching. The holes at the elbows of my sweaters and at the knees of my trousers were too big to repair. The filling of my padded jacket and quilt had fallen to the bottom, leaving places that were only two thin layers of material. Obviously, if I was to live through another winter at the **detention house,** I really needed some additional clothing. Though my past requests for clothing had always **fallen on deaf ears,** I decided to try once more and see whether I got a different response.

"Report!" I called at the door.

"What do you want?" A guard's footsteps stopped outside my cell, and the little window in the door was pushed open.

I held my sweater out to show her the holes and said, "The weather is getting cold. My clothes and quilt are so worn out that they are no longer warm. Please look at this. You can see that I really do need warm clothes for the winter."

"How long have you been here already? How many years altogether?"

"This will be my sixth winter here. I came in September 1966. My clothes were not new then and now they are no longer warm," I said. After being confined for so long I was determined to live until I was released. Probably my voice showed my anxiety. This seemed to annoy her. She closed the window and walked away.

(9)   For several days I repeated my request for warm clothing and quilts to

Revolutionaries: The young people who joined Mao's Cultural Revolution in 1966. The Revolutionaries tried to destroy old Chinese culture and traditions.
detention house: a place similar to a jail or prison where political prisoners were kept
fallen on deaf ears: If something has "fallen on deaf ears," it has not been heard, or it is being ignored.

each guard who came on duty. A week passed, and then another. The weather got colder and colder. I decided to try once more.

"Report!" I called.

"What do you want?" a guard asked through the closed door.

"I want to make a request for warm clothes. My winter clothes are worn out. Please come into the cell and look at them. I'm so afraid I might get ill again this winter if I do not get some warm clothes," I said.

She unlocked the cell door, came in, and examined my clothes and the quilt. Then she said, "I'll report to the authorities. Would you like to borrow some prison clothes for now?"

The thought of wearing prison clothes filled me with horror, because it seemed like the end of my dignity and independence. "No, thank you. I do not want to borrow prison clothes. The government is holding my assets. I want to ask permission to use some of my own money to buy some clothes," I said, deliberately emphasizing the words "my own money."

"That wouldn't do at all. We'll report your request to higher authorities and make sure you get some warm clothes when it gets really cold. Now go and study our Great Leader Chairman Mao's books."

(10)   A week later something strange occurred, a large bundle was brought to my cell by a male guard. After I had signed the receipt, he locked the door and left. I took the bundle to my bed and untied it. To my great astonishment, I found my daughter Meiping's padded jacket, heavy winter coat, two sweaters, woolen underwear, and the winter quilt for her bed. Among the clothes were several towels and a cup she used for tea. The towels looked exactly the same as they had in 1966. The padded jacket was new in 1966, and it still looked new now. I picked up the cup and found it was stained faintly brown inside. It had not been washed and the tea had dried in the cup.

(11)   My heart beat faster and faster as I examined each article and realized that this was a message of disaster. I could not help thinking that something terrible had happened to my daughter after I was arrested. She had probably died. That was why the clothes had not been worn and the towels still looked fresh and new. Perhaps her death had happened so suddenly and unexpectedly that she didn't have time to wash her teacup. My legs were shaking so violently that I had to sit down.

(12)   Then I started to think and the truth became clear. The detention house where I was kept allowed families to send prisoners clothing and necessities on the fifth day of each month. It was always a sad day as I listened to the

guards carrying parcels to other prisoners but never to me. At first, I wondered why my daughter never sent me anything. I missed not having contact with her through monthly parcels, but I was glad she was spared the unpleasant task of coming to the prison gate and waiting for hours to hand over a parcel. Now, deep in my heart, I knew that the real reason I had never received any parcels was that Meiping had died.

Comprehension Check

Check your understanding of the reading selections by marking these sentences true (*T*) or false (*F*).

___ 1. The main reason Nien Cheng was sent to prison was because she was wealthy—a member of the capitalist class.
___ 2. Mao Zedong's policies brought families and friends closer together.
___ 3. Nien Cheng had been a spy for the Kuomintang government.
___ 4. The Sun Yatsen Memorial is in Beijing, China.
___ 5. Nien Cheng was confined in a detention house for more than six years.
___ 6. At first, Cheng's requests for warm clothes and bedding were ignored.
___ 7. The government took all of Cheng's property when she was sent to prison.
___ 8. Meiping's things looked new and unused when Cheng got them.
___ 9. Prisoners were allowed to get parcels from their families once a month.
___ 10. Meiping sent her mother a parcel every month.

Critical Thinking

Answer these questions by yourself. Then work with two or three other students to discuss the questions. Decide on a group answer to each question. Be prepared to explain your group answers to the class.

1. How did Communism and Mao's policies affect human relationships?
2. Cheng was accused of being a Kuomintang spy. What reasons were given for this accusation? Do you think the accusation was reasonable? Explain why or why not.
3. Cheng finally concluded that her daughter was dead. Explain how she reached this conclusion.

Word Study

 University Word List Vocabulary

asset	discern	intense
authorize (authorities)	elaborate	material
cell	episode	obvious (obviously)
confine	expose	occur
deliberate (deliberately)	horror	policy
detriment (detrimental)	inhibit	respond (response)

Understanding Words

Word Parts

Exercise 1: Prefixes

Study the prefixes *pro-* and *anti-* in the following sentences. Notice that these prefixes are sometimes used with a hyphen.

- Big business is <u>pronuclear</u> because nuclear energy is one of the cheapest, cleanest forms of energy currently available.

- Greenpeace held an <u>antinuclear</u> rally at the site of the proposed nuclear plant. Hundreds of people protested against building another power plant.

- The young woman was strongly <u>pro-choice.</u> She believed that every woman should be able to choose whether or not to have an abortion.

- The usual treatment for a sprained ankle is to apply ice, take an <u>anti-inflammatory</u> drug like aspirin or ibuprofen, and stay off the injured leg.

What do you think the prefixes *pro-* and *anti-*mean? Write your answers on the lines provided.

pro- means _____

anti- means _____

Add the prefixes *pro-* or *anti-* to the following words. Then complete each of the following sentences with the correct new word. Use your dictionary if necessary.

trust   American   freeze   abortion   war   family

1. Thousands of young people staged an _____ demonstration outside the Capitol building to protest against America's involvement in the war.

2. The outcome of the Microsoft _____ case could eventually affect millions of computer users.

3. As working mothers make up more of the labor force, companies are having to adopt _____ policies.

4. _____ is added to a car engine before winter to prevent it from freezing in very cold weather.

5. _____ activists believe that women should be able to obtain safe and legal abortions.

6. Many individuals who wanted their country to adopt a more democratic form of government were also strongly _____.

Exercise 2: Suffixes

The suffix *-ment* means *the state or condition resulting from an action, the means or agent of an action,* or *the process of an action.* Add the suffix *-ment* to each of the words given here. Use one of the newly formed words to complete each of the following sentences. Use your dictionary if necessary.

achieve   assess   confine   discern   invest

1. Her _____ in the detention house lasted for nearly seven years.

2. It takes real _____ to understand who is your true friend and who is not.

3. According to the _____, the property taxes on the house would be over $6,000 a year.

4. Marshall's greatest _____ in civil rights was his victory in the case of *Brown v. Topeka Board of Education*.

5. Careful saving and _____ over a period of twenty-five years allowed him to retire from work at age fifty.

Exercise 3: Roots

The word *common* comes from the Latin root *communis*, meaning *shared (by a group)*. The following words also come from the same root.

communal   community   communist
commune   communism   communing

Look at the way the underlined words are used in the sentences. Match each word with its definition.

1. In the 1960s many young people went to live and work on communal farms.
2. The food grown on these farms was sold to provide an income as well as feed those who lived at the commune.
3. The community center provides sports facilities, a swimming pool, classes, and a meeting room for all the people living in the town.
4. The original theory of communism proposed that private ownership of property be eliminated. All individuals in a society would own goods in common and have equal access to them.
5. Mao wanted all Chinese to share in the land and resources of China, but in reality, communist China was different. All farms and factories were owned by the government, and the people of China worked as laborers for the state-owned businesses.
6. Many people hike in the woods or mountains because they enjoy communion with nature.

___ 1. communal   a. the area where a group of people live

___ 2. commune   b. a person who advocates communism

___ 3. community   c. participated in, shared, and used in common by a group of people

___ 4. communism   d. sharing or fellowship with a person or place

___ 5. communist   e. a community where people live and work together, sharing the ownership and use of goods

___ 6. communion   f. a totalitarian type of government where the state owns all means of production (factories, etc.)

Word Relationships

Exercise 4: Synonyms

Match each word on the left with its synonym. Then write another synonym for each word on the long line provided. Use your dictionary if necessary.

___ 1. assets   _____   a. complicated

___ 2. deliberate   _____   b. terror

___ 3. elaborate   _____   c. fabric

___ 4. expose   _____   d. possessions

___ 5. horror   _____   e. reveal

___ 6. inhibit   _____   f. intentional

___ 7. material   _____   g. procedure

___ 8. policy   _____   h. restrain

Exercise 5: Collocations

Match items 1 through 6 with their common collocations (i.e., with the words with which these items are likely to be found) by writing the combinations on the lines following items 1 through 6.

choice	lie	movie
government	monetary	story

1. assets

_____

2. deliberate

_____

3. elaborate

_____

4. horror

_____

5. obvious

_____

6. policy

_____

Word Forms

Exercise 6: Word Forms

Complete each sentence with the correct word.

1. The lawyer was _____ to sign legal documents for his client.
   authority   authorities   authorized   authorization

2. The only _____ sign of Grandmother's age was her snow white hair.
   discern   discernible   discernment   discerning

3. We now know that _____ to the sun will damage the skin and may cause cancer.
   expose   exposé   exposure   exposed

4. The prison food was _____, but prisoners had to eat it or starve.
   horror   horrify   horrific   horrible

5. He is extremely _____; money is more important to him than anything else.

   material   materialistic   materialism   immaterial

6. The government _____ to the demonstration by sending in armed soldiers.

   responded   response   responsive   respondent

Understanding Words in Sentences

Exercise 7: Word Meanings in Context

Find the words in the reading passages that have the following meanings and write these words on the lines provided. The number in parentheses is the number of the paragraph where the word occurs.

1. restrained; held back or impeded (1)   _____

2. knowledgeable; clever; bright (2)   _____

3. clearly; apparently (8)   _____

4. reply; reaction; answer (8)   _____

5. imprisoned; held; detained (8)   _____

6. intentionally; consciously (9)   _____

7. happened; took place (10)   _____

8. horrible; awful (11)   _____

Using Words in Communication

Exercise 8: Listening

Listen to the texts on the audiotape until you understand them. Then circle the correct answers.

1. According to the text, which one of these sentences is true?
    a. People were questioned about their friends and relatives.
    b. Relatives and friends wrote to Nien while she was in prison.
    c. Nien was never asked questions about her friends or family.

2. What did Nien and her husband do in 1949?
    a. They returned to Taiwan.
    b. They joined the Kuomintang.
    c. They remained in mainland China.

3. Nien's brother supposedly
    a. lived near the Foreign Trade Institute in Beijing.
    b. wanted to visit the Sun Yatsen Memorial.
    c. first tried to deny everything but later confessed.

4. According to the text, which one of these sentences is *not* true?
    a. Receiving the parcel made Nien very happy.
    b. Nien was afraid something terrible had happened to her daughter.
    c. The clothes and towels looked new, but the teacup was dirty.

 Exercise 9: Minimal Pairs

Listen to each pair of words. One of the words in each pair will be repeated a second time. Circle the word you hear repeated a second time.

1. asset	assert		5. expose	expert
2. cell	sill		6. horror	error
3. confine	confirm		7. intense	intend
4. discern	design		8. occur	recur

Exercise 10: Speaking

Read the following questions. Think carefully about the questions and then write down short answers. (If you are not comfortable giving personal answers to these questions, write about how someone you know well—a close relative or a good friend—would answer them.) Discuss these questions and your answers with a classmate. Refer to your notes if necessary.

1. What issue or idea do you feel very strongly about? (For example: discrimination, protecting the environment, or religious freedom)

2. Why do you feel this idea or issue is important?

3. What actions would you be willing to take in support or defense of this issue? What actions have you actually taken already?

4. What actions would you be unwilling to take?

5. Would you be willing to go to prison for this idea or issue? Why or why not?

Exercise 11: Reading

Throughout history men and women have been sent to prison for their political, religious, or moral beliefs. These people are often referred to as "political prisoners" or "prisoners of conscience." Here are the names of some well-known political prisoners.

Daw Aung San Suu Kyi (Myanmar)
Pramodeya Ananta Toer (Indonesia)
Wei Jingsheng (China)
Nelson Mandela (South Africa)
Aleksandr Solzhenitsyn (Soviet Union)
Martin Luther King, Jr. (United States)
Mumia Abu-Jamal (United States)

Go to the library to find information about one of these people or another person who interests you. If you want to, try to find out about a political prisoner in your own country. Consult recent encyclopedia yearbooks, the library catalogs, and periodicals or ask the reference librarian to help you locate information. You may also want to look on the Internet by using a web browser like "InfoSeek." Be prepared to give a three- to five-minute presentation about the person you choose.

Try to include the following information in your presentation.

1. Biographical information: the person's name, age, place of birth, occupation, and so on.
2. Why is he or she in prison? Has this person been accused of a crime? Is the individual in prison for protesting against something?
3. How long has this person been in prison? Will he or she be put on trial? Does this individual expect to be released from prison?
4. Is this person a member of a special group or organization? What is the purpose of this group?
5. What form of government exists in the country where the person is imprisoned?
6. What is your own view regarding the issue (apartheid, human rights, etc.) that sent the person to prison?

Exercise 12: Writing

Write a one to two page essay that answers the following questions.

Many forms of government exist today: democracies, socialist governments, communist governments, parliamentary governments, monarchies, dictatorships. Choose a country that you are very interested in. What kind of government exists in this country today? In your opinion, what are the strengths of this type of government? What are the weaknesses of this type of government? Do you think this type of government could be improved? How?

Unit 3
Jon Krakauer

Vocabulary Preview

Preview 1

Complete each sentence with the most suitable word.

accumulated   elevation   maintain   process   survey

1. Climbing the Hillary Step was a very slow _____, and Jon worried that he might run out of oxygen.

2. At an _____ of 29,000 feet, the climbers needed to breathe a mixture of bottled oxygen and outside air.

3. A lot of new snow had _____, and it was likely that avalanches would occur.

4. Jon tried to _____ his calm by telling himself, "Keep it together, keep it together," over and over.

5. The summit of Mount Everest was littered with empty oxygen

   canisters and an old _____ pole.

Preview 2

Look at the way the underlined words are used in the sentences. Match each word with its definition.

1. One benefit of using oxygen is that climbers are able to go to much higher elevations.

2. The summit was littered with metal oxygen cylinders that climbers had discarded.

3. Once I sat down to rest, I felt no impulse to get up again. It was easier to remain at rest.

4. Anatoli Boukreev was an experienced guide who had climbed Everest previously, and he led the group up the Hillary Step.

5. Jon's strange visions and experiences were similar to those that other exhausted climbers had.

___ 1. benefit
___ 2. cylinders
___ 3. impulse
___ 4. previously
___ 5. similar

a. at an earlier time; before
b. a sudden urge or feeling
c. an aid; a help; an improvement
d. like; having the same features
e. metal containers with flat circular ends and long straight sides

Reading Preview: What Do You Know about Jon Krakauer and Mount Everest?

Circle the correct answer. If you don't know the answer, guess.

1. Mount Everest
    a. is the highest mountain in the world at 29,028 feet (8,848 meters)
    b. was successfully climbed by the first westerner, Sir Edmund Hillary, in 1953
    c. is considered a holy place by the people of Tibet
    d. all of the above

2. Jon Krakauer
    a. led the first successful group of American climbers up Mount Everest
    b. is a television sports reporter
    c. is a climber who has written several books about outdoor adventures
    d. died on Mount Everest on May 10, 1996

3. The Everest climbing expedition described here became famous because
    a. it was very expensive (it cost more than $65,000 per person)
    b. the group set a record for the fastest summit climb
    c. everyone made the climb without using bottled oxygen
    d. eight people—including two experienced expedition leaders—died

Adapted from *Into Thin Air: A Personal Account of the Mount Everest Disaster* by Jon Krakauer (New York: Villard Books, 1997), 179–81, 189–95.

Introduction to the Readings

Climbing **Mount Everest,** the world's tallest mountain, is the ambition of many serious mountaineers. Many excellent climbers have tried to reach the summit of Everest and succeeded. Many others have tried and failed. Many have died trying. The extreme high altitude, bitter cold, and severe weather test the physical endurance and skills of everyone who tries to climb it. Thirty or forty years ago, only the very best and most experienced climbers could attempt to climb Everest, but recently commercial "adventure tours" have made it possible for relatively inexperienced climbers to give it a try.

Jon Krakauer is an experienced climber who has written several books about mountaineering and the outdoors. His book *Into Thin Air* documents a commercial Everest expedition during 1996 that turned into a terrible disaster. The two expedition leaders, Rob Hall and Scott Fischer, and six of the climbers died on the mountain. The tragedy raised an important question about commercial climbing expeditions. Should anyone—regardless of experience and ability—who has the desire, and the money, be allowed to attempt such dangerous climbs? What do you think?

The excerpts here describe the day Krakauer's group attempted to climb to the summit of Everest.

Mount Everest: With a height of 29,028 feet (8,848 meters), Everest is the tallest mountain in the world. Mount Everest is located in the Himalayan Mountains on the border between Tibet and Nepal.

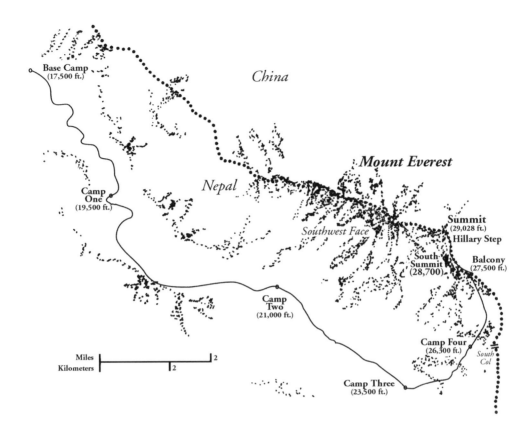

Reading 1: The Summit

(1)   Bottled oxygen does not make the top of Mount Everest feel like sea level. Climbing above the South Summit with my oxygen tank giving me just under two liters of oxygen per minute, I had to stop and take three or four breaths of air after every step. Then I'd take one more step and have to pause for another four deep breaths. This was the fastest pace I could manage. The oxygen systems we were using delivered a mixture of oxygen gas and out-side air. One of the benefits of using oxygen was that it made an elevation of 29,000 feet with gas feel like approximately 26,000 feet without gas.

(2)   Climbing along the **summit ridge,** sucking gas into my lungs, I felt a strange sense of calm. The world outside my rubber mask was bright and clear but seemed not quite real. I felt drugged and separated from the ex-ternal world. I had to remind myself over and over that there was 7,000 feet

summit ridge: a long, narrow crest at the very top of the mountain

of sky on either side of me, and that I would pay for a single wrong step with my life.

(3)   Half an hour above the South Summit I arrived at forty feet of almost vertical rock and ice known as the Hillary Step. As a serious climber, I very much wanted to lead our group up the Step. But it was clear that each of the guides felt the same way, and I was crazy to hope that one of them was going to let me, a client, take the lead. In the end, Boukreev—as the most experienced guide and the only one of us who had climbed Everest previously—claimed the honor, and he did a beautiful job of leading that section of the climb. But it was a slow process, and as he climbed toward the top I began to wonder whether I might run out of oxygen.

(4)   At the top of the Step I shared my concern with Beidleman and asked him whether he minded if I hurried ahead to the summit instead of staying to help him. **"Go for it,"** he offered. "I'll take care of the rope." Walking slowly up the last few steps to the summit, I felt as if I were underwater and moving at quarter speed. And then I found myself on top of a thin wedge of ice littered with a discarded oxygen cylinder and an old aluminum **survey pole,** with nowhere higher to climb. Far below, down a side of the mountain I had never seen, the dry, brown earth of **Tibet** stretched to the horizon.

(5)   Reaching the top of Everest is supposed to cause a feeling of intense happiness; after all, after great difficulties, I had just attained a goal I'd had since my childhood. But the summit was really only the halfway point. Any impulse I might have felt to congratulate myself was canceled by my fears of the long, dangerous descent that lay ahead.

Reading 2: The Descent

(6)   At about 4:45 P.M. I reached the Balcony—a kind of bump at 27,600 feet on the Southeast Ridge. Daylight was fading as I descended safely a few hundred feet down a broad gentle snow-filled valley, but then things began to get difficult. The route wandered through broken rock that was covered with 6 inches of new snow. Getting through this confusing, slippery area took complete concentration, which was almost impossible in my exhausted condition.

"go for it": slang for "try to do it"
survey pole: a pole used to mark the points of measurement when land is measured and marked out
Tibet: A high plateau area that is now part of southwestern China. Tibet was formerly an independent country.

Photograph of Mt. Everest courtesy of Alpine Ascents International.

(7)   The wind had erased the tracks of the climbers who had gone down before me, and I had difficulty deciding on the correct route. In 1993, a skilled
Himalayan climber had taken a wrong turn in this area and fallen to his
death. Fighting to **maintain a grip on reality,** I started talking to myself out
loud. "**Keep it together,** keep it together, keep it together," I said over and
over. "You can't afford to make a mistake here. This is very serious. Keep it
together."

(8)   I sat down to rest on a broad, sloping rock, but after a few minutes a deaf-
ening BOOM! frightened me and I got back on my feet. Enough new snow had
accumulated that I was afraid the noise had been caused by an **avalanche.**
Then there was another BOOM!, accompanied by a flash, and I realized I was
hearing the crash of thunder.

(9)   By 6:00 P.M., as the storm became a full-scale **blizzard** with driving snow
and winds blowing at more than **60 knots,** I came to a fixed rope on the snowy

maintain a grip on reality: slang for "keep an awareness of what is actually happening"
"keep it together": slang for "stay calm and reasonable, don't panic"
avalanche: A large mass of snow that falls down a mountain. Climbers and skiers are killed by avalanches
every year.
blizzard: a very heavy snowstorm, often with extremely strong winds
60 knots: A measure of the speed of the wind. One knot is a speed of about 1,852 meters/hour. Sixty knots
would be about 111 kilometers, or 69 miles/hour.

slope about 600 feet above the South **Col** (the area just above Camp Four). Wrapping the rope around my arms I continued down through the blizzard. Some minutes later I had a familiar sensation of not being able to breathe, and I realized my oxygen had once again run out. I pulled the mask from my face, left it hanging around my neck, and kept going, surprisingly unconcerned. However, without the supplemental oxygen, I moved more slowly, and I had to stop and rest more often.

(10) There are many stories about strange visions and experiences on Everest that are attributed to lack of oxygen and **fatigue.** I gradually became aware that my mind was behaving in a similar fashion, and I observed my own slide from reality with a mixture of fascination and horror. I was so exhausted that I felt detached from my body, as if I were observing myself from a few feet overhead. I imagined that I was dressed in a green sweater and business shoes. And although the windchill was more than 70 degrees below zero Fahrenheit, I felt strangely warm.

(11) At 6:30 there was only one thing between me and the safety of Camp Four: an incline of hard glassy ice that I would have to descend without a rope. The tents, no more than 650 horizontal feet away, were only sometimes visible through the snow. Worried about making a critical mistake, I sat down to rest and collect my energy before I went any further. Once I sat down I felt no impulse to get up again. It was easier to remain at rest than to cross the dangerous ice slope. I just sat there as the storm roared around me, letting my mind wander, doing nothing for perhaps 45 minutes.

(12) I was tired, and worried about getting down the slope without breaking a leg, so I tossed my backpack over the edge and hoped I could find it later. Then I stood up and started down the ice, which was as smooth and hard as the surface of a bowling ball. Fifteen difficult, tiring minutes later I was safely at the bottom of the incline. I found my pack and in another ten minutes was in the camp itself. I got into my tent with my **crampons** still on, zipped the door tight, and lay across the icy floor too tired to sit upright. For the first time I had a sense of how drained I really was: I was more exhausted than I'd ever been in my life. But I was safe. We had climbed Everest. It had been a little scary there for a while, but in the end everything had turned out great.

Col: a ridge that connects two higher elevations; a pass in the mountains
fatigue: exhaustion, tiredness
crampons: sets of spikes that are attached to the bottom of climbing boots and used for climbing on ice and in snow

(13)   It would be many hours before I learned that everything had not in fact turned out great—that nineteen men and women were **stranded** up on the mountain by the storm, caught in a desperate struggle for their lives.

Comprehension Check

Check your understanding of the reading selections by marking these sentences true (*T*) or false (*F*).

___ 1. Jon Krakauer was an experienced climber who led the expedition.
___ 2. The use of bottled oxygen makes climbing Mount Everest quite easy.
___ 3. Jon wanted to go ahead of Beidleman because he was afraid he would run out of oxygen.
___ 4. Jon didn't feel happy when he reached the summit, because he still had to make the long, dangerous descent back down the mountain.
___ 5. Until he saw the flash of lightning, Jon thought that the loud "BOOM!" he heard was caused by an avalanche.
___ 6. Extreme tiredness and lack of oxygen make some climbers see strange things.
___ 7. Jon couldn't stop to rest before crossing the ice above Camp Four because the wind was too strong.
___ 8. Nineteen people died on the Everest expedition.

Critical Thinking

Answer these questions by yourself. Then work with two or three other students to discuss the questions. Decide on a group answer to each question. Be prepared to explain your group answers to the class.

1. Should anyone—regardless of experience and ability—be allowed to attempt to climb Mount Everest? Should having the desire and the money be enough? Give the reasons why you agree or disagree.

stranded: left in a place (or situation) without any way of leaving it

2. Who is ultimately responsible for the safety of the climbers, the expedition leaders or the climbers themselves? Explain your answer.
3. How do you think the presence of less experienced climbers affects an expedition of this type? Are there any benefits or advantages to having inexperienced climbers along? Are there any disadvantages?

Word Study

 University Word List Vocabulary

accumulate	elevate (elevation)	pole
attribute	energy	previous (previously)
benefit	impulse	process
client	incline	route
cylinder	maintain	similar
drain	oxygen	survey

Understanding Words

Word Parts

Exercise 1: Prefixes

The prefixes *de-* and *dis-* are used in similar but slightly different ways. The Latin prefix *de-* means *to remove from something, to reduce, to do the opposite of,* and *to get off of.* Add the prefix *de-* to the words that follow and then match the new words with their meanings. Use your dictionary if necessary.

__ 1. activate   _____

__ 2. caffeinated   _____

__ 3. plane   _____

__ 4. value   _____

a. having the caffeine removed
b. to reduce the worth of
c. to make ineffective; to shut off
d. to exit a plane

The Latin prefix *dis-* means *to do the opposite of, to deprive of, to exclude, to expel,* and *not.* Add the prefix *dis-* to the words that follow and then match the new words with their meanings. Use your dictionary if necessary.

__ 5. approve   _____

__ 6. integrate   _____

__ 7. orient   _____

__ 8. place   _____

a. to remove from the usual or proper place
b. to destroy; to break into parts
c. to reject; to pass unfavorable judgment on
d. to confuse; to lose the sense of time, place, or identity

Exercise 2: Prefixes

Use one of the words from Exercise 1 to complete each sentence. Add endings (*-s, -ed, -ing*) where needed.

1. Many people prefer to drink _____ coffee because the caffeine in regular coffee keeps them awake at night.

2. Thousands of refugees were _____ from their homeland by the war.

3. The blowing snow made it difficult to see, and the climbers quickly became _____.

4. In the event of an emergency landing, all passengers are told to _____ through the rear exit only.

5. Falling stock prices caused the U.S. dollar to _____ sharply against major European currencies.

6. As more and more people _____ of smoking in restaurants and public places, "no smoking" areas have become more common.

7. The bomb squad was able to _____ the bomb safely before an explosion occurred.

8. Many meteors and asteroids enter the earth's atmosphere but _____ before ever hitting the ground.

Exercise 3: Suffixes

The suffix *-ance / -ence* can be added to an adjective, a noun, or a verb to form a noun. (Remember that the spelling of the word that takes the suffix may need to be altered slightly.) These new nouns usually refer to a quality or a state of being. Add the correct form of the suffix *-ance/-ence* to the words given and then use one of the new words to complete each of the following sentences. Use your dictionary if necessary.

ally	__alliance__	occur	_____
assure	_____	maintain	_____
confer	_____	persist	_____
diverge	_____	rely	_____

1. Proper care and _____ of equipment are important for safety reasons.

2. The group had a short _____ to decide who would lead the summit climb.

3. Jon's _____, his complete refusal to give up, helped him to get back to camp safely.

4. Among serious climbers, there is some _____ of opinion about the safety of commercial "adventure" tours.

5. Avalanches are a common _____ after a heavy snowfall.

6. The climbers' _____ on bottled oxygen allowed them to climb at higher elevations.

7. The two expedition leaders formed a casual _____—they agreed to assist one another whenever possible during the Everest climb.

8. There was no _____ that all of the climbers would make it to the summit of Everest.

Can you think of any other words that use *-ance / -ence* in this way? Write them here.

_____   _____   _____

Word Relationships

Exercise 4: Synonyms and Antonyms

Identify the following pairs of words as synonyms (*S*) or antonyms (*A*).

___ 1. accumulate / distribute   ___ 5. attribute / characteristic

___ 2. client / vendor   ___ 6. drain / fill

___ 3. energy / fuel   ___ 7. incline / lean

___ 4. route / path   ___ 8. elevate / lower

Understanding Words in Sentences

Exercise 5: Using Words Correctly

The word *accumulate* means *to gather or pile up, to increase in quantity or number.* The word *elevate* means to *raise up* or *to increase abnormally.* Read the sentences that follow and decide whether or not each word in italics has been used correctly in terms of meaning. Mark the sentence correct (*C*) or incorrect (*I*). If the word in italics has been used incorrectly, cross it out and replace it with a better word.

___ 1. Six or seven inches of new snow had *accumulated* during the night.

___ 2. Experienced climbers have *elevated* a lot of knowledge about proper climbing techniques, safety, and first aid.

___ 3. Stress and fatigue can cause *accumulated* blood pressure.

___ 4. College students *accumulate* a lot of textbooks over four years.

___ 5. Climbing at higher *elevations* requires the use of oxygen.

___ 6. Public buildings are required to have *elevates* that can be used easily by disabled persons.

Exercise 6: Word Meanings in Context

Reread the following passages from the reading selections. Then complete the sentences or answer the questions by circling the letter of the correct choice.

1. As a serious climber, I very much wanted to lead our group up the Step. But it was clear that each of the guides felt the same way, and I was crazy to hope that one of them was going to let me, a client, take the lead. In the end, Boukreev—as the most experienced guide and the only one of us who had climbed Everest previously—claimed the honor.

   Why didn't Jon lead the group up the Step?
   a. He had never climbed Everest before.
   b. The most experienced guide led the group.
   c. He was afraid of making a mistake.

2. Climbing the Step was a slow process, and as Boukreev climbed toward the top I began to wonder whether I might run out of oxygen. At the top of the Step I shared my concern with Beidleman and asked him whether he minded if I hurried ahead to the summit instead of staying to help him. "Go for it," he offered. "I'll take care of the rope."

   Jon was concerned that
   a. Boukreev was climbing too slowly
   b. he would run out of oxygen before he got to the summit
   c. Beidleman couldn't take care of the rope alone

3. Reaching the top of Everest is supposed to cause a feeling of intense happiness; after all, after great difficulties, I had just attained a goal I'd had since my childhood. But the summit was really only the halfway point. Any impulse I might have felt to congratulate myself was canceled by my fears of the long, dangerous descent that lay ahead.

   How did Jon feel when he reached the top of Everest?
   a. He felt afraid because he still had to go back down the mountain.
   b. He felt intensely happy.
   c. He wanted to congratulate himself for attaining a goal he'd had since his childhood.

4. There are many stories about strange visions and experiences on Everest that are attributed to lack of oxygen and fatigue. I gradually became aware that my mind was behaving in a similar fashion, and I observed my own slide from reality with a mixture of fascination and horror.

   Jon was
   a. horrified by what other high altitude climbers had experienced
   b. surprised by his own strange visions and experiences
   c. aware that he was beginning to have strange visions and experiences

5. At 6:30 there was only one thing between me and the safety of Camp Four: an incline of hard glassy ice that I would have to descend without a rope. The tents, no more than 650 horizontal feet away, were only sometimes visible through the snow.

   Why were the last 650 feet dangerous to cross?
   a. It was dark out, and Jon couldn't see anything.
   b. The slope was icy, and Jon had to cross it without a rope.
   c. Jon was exhausted and hallucinating.

Using Words in Communication

 Exercise 7: Listening

Listen to each text on the audiotape and then summarize it in two or three sentences. Try to use at least one study word in your summary.

1. _____

   _____

   _____

2. _____

   _____

   _____

3. _____

_____

_____

4. _____

_____

_____

Exercise 8: Minimal Pairs

Listen to each pair of words. One of the words in each pair will be repeated a second time. Circle the word you hear repeated a second time.

1.	client	pliant	6.	drain	rain
2.	debate	rebate	7.	previous	devious
3.	pole	bowl	8.	route	drought
4.	labor	neighbor	9.	stress	dress
5.	context	contact	10.	schemes	screams

Exercise 9: Discussion

Work with another student. Choose and rank the eight items that you think would be the most useful if you got lost and were stranded overnight in the mountains.

___ waterproof matches   ___ a map
___ a tent   ___ a mirror
___ two chocolate bars and three oranges ___ a canteen of water
___ a sleeping bag   ___ a knife
___ a fishing pole   ___ a first aid kit
___ insect repellent   ___ a flashlight
___ a cell phone   ___ a cylinder of oxygen
___ a fifty foot rope   ___ pencil and paper
___ a compass   ___ a bottle of brandy

After you have finished, show your list to another pair of students and explain why you and your partner chose these items.

Exercise 10: Reading

Read the text that follows and fill in the blanks with one of these words. Then answer the questions.

alternative	elevated	inclines	responded
attributes	energetic	injury	shifting
conservative	expose	physically	similar
elaborate			

Extreme Sports

Extreme sports, such as skateboarding, snowboarding, in-line skating, bicycle stunt riding, and rock climbing, are increasingly popular with young

Americans. In cities across the country, _____ young men and women can be seen carrying skateboards or strapping on knee pads and roller blades and heading to the nearest skate park.

    Skateboarding is perhaps the most popular extreme sport among an important group of consumers: young American males. Advertisers have

_____ to this popularity, and skateboarders now appear in ads for everything from snack foods to telephone services. Skateboarding is so popular that many communities have built their own skate parks. The city of Escondido, California, recently opened a two million dollar sports center that

features an _____ 20,000 foot skate park—the largest in the country. Skate parks are growing increasingly sophisticated, too, with a variety of

_____, _____ ramps, pipes, and bowls designed to test even the best skateboarders.

    Snowboarding is _____ to skateboarding in that participants do stunts with a flat board, but a snowboard has no wheels. Snowboarding also requires one thing that skateboarding does not: snow. Many serious athletes actually participate in both sports, and there are a number of "tricks" or moves that can be done on either type of board. Some snowboard moves are also taken from downhill skiing: the giant slalom and "big air" jumping are two examples. However, compared to skateboarding and skiing, snowboarding can be a very risky sport. More than one young athlete has

had his or her snowboarding career ended by a severe _____ or

death.

So, what makes these _____ demanding sports so appealing?

Why are young people _____ away from more _____ , tra-

ditional sports to these risky _____ sports? A survey of young

X-tremers, as they call themselves, may give us some insight. Most love

extreme sports because they are challenging and exciting. These sports

_____ the participants to risk, and only those athletes with physi-

cal strength, coordination, balance, timing, luck, and nerves of steel can

meet the challenge. Do these sound like _____ that you have? If

so, maybe you should give an extreme sport a try. But please be careful!

Questions

1. Name several extreme sports. Which of these is currently the most
   popular in the United States?
2. What things mentioned in the article indicate how popular skateboarding has become?
3. According to the article, which sport is the most dangerous, skateboarding, snowboarding, or skiing? Do you agree or disagree? Why?
4. In your opinion, why are young people attracted to extreme sports?

Exercise 11: Writing

Choose topic *a* or *b* and write a three to four paragraph essay.

a. Select one of the Critical Thinking questions on pages 47–48 and write
   an essay that answers the question.
b. Select one of the extreme sports mentioned in Exercise 10 and write an
   essay that describes the sport and explains why you find it interesting.

Review Unit 1

I. Choose the correct word from the list on the left to go with each meaning. (In each set, you will not use two of the words.)

Example:

1. align
2. intervene
3. indigenous
4. impact
5. invade

<u>4</u> violent blow
<u>3</u> native
<u>5</u> attack

Set A

1. absorb
2. emphasize
3. confine
4. expose
5. accumulate

<u>4</u> uncover
<u>5</u> collect
<u>2</u> stress

Set B

1. previous
2. detrimental
3. elaborate
4. conservative
5. alternative

<u>5</u> option
<u>2</u> harmful
<u>1</u> prior

Set C

1. circumstance
2. asset
3. route
4. process
5. episode

<u>4</u> method
<u>1</u> condition
<u>3</u> path

II. Identify the following pairs of words as synonyms (*S*) or antonyms (*A*).

S 1. client/customer   S 5. obvious/evident
A 2. similar/different   S 6. inhibit/restrain
S 3. incline/slope   A 7. injure/heal
S 4. deliberate/careless   A 8. secure/release

III. Match each word on the left with a word on the right with which it often collocates.

I 1. approximate   a. assure
G 2. personal   b. shift
C 3. employee   c. policy
J 4. bathtub   d. composure
D 5. maintain   e. benefits
E 6. government   f. property
H 7. horror   g. cell
B 8. night   h. movie
                          i. measurement
                          j. drain

IV. Complete each sentence with the correct word.

1. Bobby Riggs thought that, because he was a man, he was

   _____ of an easy victory against Billie Jean King.
   assure   assured   reassured   assurance

2. After nearly seven years, the _____ allowed Nien Cheng
   to have additional clothing and blankets—those that had belonged
   to her daughter.
   authority   authorize   authorities   authorization

3. It was snowing so hard that we couldn't see, and it was difficult to

   _____ where the path was.
   discern   discerning   discerned   discernment

4. Terrible storms are a common _____ in the mountains.
   occur   occurred   occurring   occurrence

5. People living in capitalist societies appear very _____ compared to those living in communist societies.

   material   (materialistic)   immaterial   materialize

6. Mount Everest's high _____ is a tremendous challenge for climbers.

   elevate   elevator   elevated   (elevation)

V. Complete each analogy with one of the words given here.

cell	impulse	rhythm
cylinder	intense	survey

1. slow : quick :: plan : *Impulse*

2. element : atom :: body : *cell*

3. weak : mild :: strong : *Intense*

4. violin : melody :: drum : *rhythm*

5. square : cube :: circle : *cylinder*

6. goods : inventory :: land : *Survey*

VI. Complete each sentence with one of the words given here.

accuracy	episode	energy
atmosphere	attribute	oxygen

1. Water, or H_2O, is composed of two elements: hydrogen and *oxygen*.

2. The TV program was divided into *episode* that were shown on three consecutive evenings.

3. Computers allow us to do many types of work—writing, calculating, even drawing—with greater *accuracy* and speed.

4. Some say that her greatest personal *attribute* is her intelligence; others say that it is her courage.

5. The earth's _atmosphere_ is composed of a mixture of gases that includes oxygen, carbon dioxide, and nitrogen.

6. The E in the formula $E = MC^2$ stands for _energy_, the M is for mass, and the C represents the speed of light.

Unit 4
Katharine Graham

Vocabulary Preview

Preview 1

Complete each sentence with the most suitable word.

comments   executive   investigating   journalism   crisis

1. Since 1993, Katharine Graham has been chairperson of the

   _____ committee of the Washington Post Company.
2. The best we could do under the circumstances was to keep

   _____, to look everywhere for hard evidence.

3. The Watergate scandal created a national _____ that spanned
   an entire decade.

4. The secretary had heard plenty of _____ that high-ranking
   members of the president's staff were out to hurt Graham.

5. Watergate also changed the way _____ and journalists are
   viewed.

Preview 2

Look at the way the underlined words are used in the sentences. Match
each word with its definition.

1. Sir Isaac Newton used Picard's measurements of the earth to <u>verify</u> his
   theory of gravitation.
2. Some people still believe that the courts should not <u>intervene</u> in arguments between family members.
3. Craters are often formed by the <u>impact</u> of heavenly bodies on the
   earth's surface.
4. Wilson refused to <u>deviate</u> from the course he felt God intended him to
   follow.
5. In his bumbling manner, Friar Lawrence <u>contributes</u> to the deaths of
   Romeo and Juliet.

___ 1. verify   a. to be an important factor in
___ 2. intervene   b. to prove the truth of
___ 3. impact   c. to move away from the accepted or usual
___ 4. deviate   d. to come between
___ 5. contribute   e. forceful, violent contact

Reading Preview

This unit is about journalism, the field of producing, gathering, and reporting news for the media (whether newspaper, television, radio, news magazines). In particular, it is about the stresses and concerns faced by a publisher in covering a huge national story. It is also about the personalities and dedication of the two journalists who brought the story before the American public. The publisher is Katharine Graham; the newspaper, the *Washington Post;* and the two reporters, Bob Woodward and Carl Bernstein.

In order to understand the reading selections, you need to familiarize yourself with the story of the Watergate **scandal.** The next two sections will help you understand the reading passages. The first section, Guide Questions, will have you start thinking about the topic. The second section is a time line of events surrounding Watergate. Discuss both sections with several classmates to make sure that you understand why Graham was so anxious and careful about the role her paper was playing as the story was breaking.

Guide Questions

1. Has there ever been a huge political scandal in your country?
2. Was the press able to discuss and report on this scandal freely?
3. Could individuals exposed by the scandal sue for **libel**?
4. In your country, how do people defend themselves against libel?

Adapted from *Personal History* by Katharine Graham (New York: Alfred A. Knopf, 1997), 468–72 and 506–8.
scandal: shameful occurrence or event that goes against the accepted rules of society
libel: anything that is said or written untruthfully to harm a person

Washington Post *Time Line of Watergate Events*

June 1972	Five men are arrested as they are trying to break into the Democratic National Committee Headquarters at the Watergate apartment complex in Washington, D.C.
August 1972	A check for $25,000, contributed to the Nixon campaign, ends up in the bank account of one of the **burglars.** When asked about the check, John Mitchell, who had been attorney general and was now head of the Nixon reelection campaign, denies any administration link to the check or the burglary.
September 1972	The *Post* reveals that Mitchell, while serving as attorney general, controlled a secret Republican fund that he used to finance intelligence-gathering operations against the Democrats.
October 1972	FBI agents establish that the Watergate break-in is part of a huge campaign of spying and sabotage conducted by high-level Republicans in an effort to get Nixon reelected.
November 1972	Nixon is reelected in a national **landslide.**
January 1973	Two Nixon aides, G. Gordon Liddy and James McCord, are convicted of conspiracy, burglary, and **wiretapping** in the Watergate incident.
April 1973	The highest-ranking members of Nixon's staff, H. R. Haldeman, his chief of staff, and John Ehrlichman, his domestic adviser, as well as Attorney General Richard Kleindienst, resign over the scandal. White House **counsel** John Dean is fired.
May 1973	The **Senate** Watergate Committee begins to hold nationally televised **hearings.**
June 1973	In the Senate hearings, John Dean reveals to the committee that he has discussed the Watergate **cover-up** with the president at least thirty-five times. Alexander Butterfield, former presidential appointment secretary, reveals at the hearings that, since 1971, Nixon has recorded all telephone calls and conversations that took place in his office. The Senate Watergate Committee subpoenas the presidential tapes. Nixon refuses to turn over the tapes from his office to the Senate Watergate Committee.

burglars: thieves; robbers
landslide: an overwhelming victory, especially in an election
wiretapping: secret interception of wire communications through the use of miniature radio transmitters and a variety of radio-receiving and voice-recording equipment
counsel: legal adviser; attorney
Senate hearings: meetings of an investigative committee, made up of U.S. senators, to determine whether illegal activities have taken place
cover-up: an attempt to hide an immoral or corrupt act

October 1973	The "Saturday Night Massacre": Nixon fires **Special Prosecutor** Archibald Cox and abolishes the office of special prosecutor. The president's newly appointed attorney general, Elliott Lee Richardson, and deputy attorney general William Ruckleshaus resign when they are asked to fire the special prosecutor. Pressure to **impeach** the president mounts in Congress.
December 1973	The White House attorneys acknowledge an 18 1/2 minute gap in one of the **subpoenaed** tapes. Judge Sirica tells the public about the gap.
April 1974	The **House Judiciary Commitee** subpoenas the tapes. The White House releases 1,254 pages of **edited transcripts** of the Nixon tapes to the committee, but the committee insists that the tapes themselves must be turned over.
May 1974	Nixon begins listening to the tapes again, and again refuses to turn them over.
July 1974	The Supreme Court **unanimously** rejects the president's claim of **executive privilege** and orders him to turn over the 64 tapes of recordings of White House conversations. Four articles of impeachment pass in the House.
August 1974	Richard Nixon becomes the first U.S. president to resign. Vice President Gerald Ford becomes president and soon after **pardons** Nixon of all charges related to Watergate.

special prosecutor: a person appointed to the special task of investigating wrongdoing and bringing charges against the wrongdoers

to impeach: To begin proceedings to remove the president from office. In the U.S., the House of Representatives begins the impeachment proceedings, and the Senate acts as judge.

subpoenaed: ordered to present oneself or materials in one's possession to a court of law

House Judiciary Committee: the congressional committee empowered to start impeachment proceedings against the president

edited transcripts: written texts of tapes that had been altered in order to leave out evidence that would incriminate the president

unanimously: in total agreement, without a vote of dissent

executive privilege: the president's privilege not to disclose information when such disclosure would harm his ability to carry out his presidential functions

pardon: to legally release from punishment

Introduction to the Readings

By breaking the story of the Pentagon Papers, the Defense Department's secret history of the Vietnam War, and by breaking the Watergate story that brought down President Richard Nixon, Katharine Graham succeeded in turning the family-owned *Washington Post* from a hometown newspaper to a publication of huge national and international consequence and prestige. Graham, who, after her husband's death in 1963, took over as president of the *Post,* has since become a legend in American journalism and American business. In 1995, she was named one of the one hundred most powerful women in the world. Since 1993, she has been chairman of the executive committee of the Washington Post Company, an enterprise that currently owns both the *Post* and *Newsweek Magazine.*

The four readings here are excerpts from Katharine Graham's account of the scandal as recorded in her **Pulitzer Prize**–winning autobiography *Personal History.* The first excerpt is Graham's description of Bob Woodward and Carl Bernstein, the two reporters mainly responsible for investigating and writing about Watergate. The remaining three are about Graham's efforts to ensure that her paper would not be sued for libel and that everything being printed in the *Post* was 100 percent true.

Reading 1: Bob Woodward and Carl Bernstein— Key Reporters on the Story

(1)   Woodward had come to us fresh from the Navy. Having been accepted by Harvard Law School, he had chosen instead to pursue journalism as a career. He so much wanted to work for the *Post* that the managing editor had instructed his deputy to put Woodward on for two weeks—without pay— and to look at his copy every night to see what he could do. Not one of the seventeen stories that Bob wrote during those two weeks was ever printed and, at the end of the trial period, the deputy confidently declared that Woodward was a bright and good guy but lacked the skills needed for being a newspaper man—in short, he was hopeless, and would be too much trouble to train. The deputy told Woodward to get some experience and come back

Pulitzer Prize: A series of prizes awarded for outstanding public service and achievement in American journalism, literature, and music. The prize is highly valued.

in a year. So Bob went off and got a job in a nearby newspaper and, after several months, he began to call the *Post* editor back until the editor finally decided to hire him. From the beginning Bob distinguished himself at the *Post*.

(2) Carl Bernstein, on the other hand, had been at the *Post* since the fall of 1966 but had not distinguished himself. He was a good writer but his poor work habits were well known throughout the **city room** even then. In fact, one thing that stood in the way of Carl's being put on the story was that **Ben** was about to fire him. Carl was notorious for an irresponsible expense account and numerous other delinquencies—including having rented a car and abandoned it in a parking lot, presenting the company with an enormous bill. But Carl, looking over Bob's shoulder while he reworked parts of the text, immediately **got hooked on** this strange story and was off and running. Top editors were told that Carl was pursuing the Watergate story with verve, working hard, and contributing a great deal. It was Carl, early on, in fact, who made the first connection of the crisp $100 bills in the pockets of the burglars to the money raised for the Nixon campaign. Bradlee decided to keep him on the story.

(3) Woodward and Bernstein clearly were the key reporters on the story— so much so that we began to refer to them collectively as "Woodstein." In September of 1972, their first report on what was to become "The Watergate Scandal" appeared in the *Post*. Two weeks later, a **seminal** article, also written by them appeared on page one of the *Post*. They had dug up information that there was a secret fund, controlled by John Mitchell and four other people, which was to be used to gather intelligence on the Democrats. Thus the story reached a new level, involving Mitchell himself, not only in his new role in the campaign, but when he was still attorney general, since Woodward and Bernstein had unearthed Mitchell-authorized expenditures for the fund from the previous year.

city room: a room at the newspaper where news stories are gathered and written
Ben: Ben was Ben Bradlee, the managing (top) editor of the *Post* at the time.
got hooked on: became very interested in
seminal: containing or contributing seeds for later development

Reading 2: The *Washington Post*—Its Role in the Watergate Scandal

Photograph of Dustin Hoffman and Robert Redford from *All the President's Men* courtesy of the *Museum of Modern Art/Film Stills Archive.*

(4)   By October of 1972, five months into the scandal, I was feeling stressed. The constant attacks on us by the Committee to Re-elect the President and by people throughout the Nixon administration were effective. During these months, the pressures on the *Post* to stop writing about Watergate were intense and uncomfortable, to say the least. But, unbelievable as the revelations coming out of our investigations were, the strong evidence of their accuracy is part of what kept us going.

(5)   Many of my friends were puzzled about our reporting. Readers also were writing to me, accusing the *Post* of **ulterior motives,** bad journalism, and lack of patriotism. It was a particularly lonely moment for us at the paper. Other organizations were beginning to report the story but we were so far ahead that they could not catch up; Woodward and Bernstein had most of the **sources**

ulterior motives: self-serving reasons for acting in a certain way
sources: In this context, sources are the people from whom reporters get their information.

to themselves. The **wire services** sent out our stories, but most papers either didn't run them or buried them somewhere toward the back pages. **Howard** used to get on the phone to his editor friends around the country to tell them they were missing a big story but they didn't jump on it. I sometimes privately thought: If this is such a great story, then why isn't anyone else writing about it?

(6)   Bearing the full weight of presidential and public disapproval is always disturbing. Sometimes I wondered if we could survive four more years of this kind of strain, of the pressures of living with an administration determined to harm us. I couldn't help thinking about what condition we'd all be in—including the paper—at the end of it. The best we could do under such an attack, I felt, was to keep investigating, to look everywhere for hard evidence, to get the details right, and to report accurately what we found.

Reading 3: Applying Rigorous Journalistic Standards

(7)   Peter Peterson, Nixon's secretary of commerce, remained a friend of mine throughout our reporting of Watergate. Having heard plenty of comments that the White House was out to "get" me, Peter came to my office one day to say, "Kay, I don't know what the truth is, but there is a group of very angry people who feel you are out to get them. I hope you are using **rigorous** journalistic standards. If you are wrong, it's serious; they will get you." I assured him that I heard what he was saying—and that we were being careful.

(8)   Indeed, we were. We always did our best to be careful and responsible, especially when we were carrying the burden of the Watergate reporting. From the beginning, the editors had made up their minds to handle the story with more than the usual exacting, precise attention to fairness and detail. They laid down certain rules which were followed by everyone.

First, every bit of information attributed to an unnamed source had to be supported by at least one other, independent source. Particularly at the start of Watergate, we had to rely heavily on confidential sources, but at every step we double-checked every bit of material before printing it; where possible, we had three or even more sources for the story.

wire service: An agency, such as the Associated Press (AP) or United Press International (UPI), that gathers, writes, and distributes news from around the nation or world to newspapers, radio and television broadcasters, and government agencies. A wire service does not *publish* news; it just *supplies* news to its subscribers.
Howard: one of the senior editors of the *Post*
rigorous: strict; severe; accurate

Second, we ran nothing that was reported by any other newspaper, television, radio station, or other media outlet unless it was independently verified and confirmed by our own reporters.

Third, every word of every story was read by at least one of the senior editors before it went into print, with a top editor thoroughly checking each story before it ran. As any journalist knows, these are rigorous tests.

(9)   Yet despite the care I knew everyone was taking, I was still worried. No matter how careful we were, there was always the possibility that we were wrong, being set up, misled. Ben would repeatedly reassure me by saying that having the story almost to ourselves gave us the luxury of not having to rush into print. It meant that we could be obsessive about checking out everything. There were many times when we delayed publishing something until the tests had been met. There were times when something just didn't seem to hold up and, accordingly, was not published, and there were a number of instances where we withheld something not sufficiently verified that turned out later to be true. This attention to detail and to playing by our own strict rules allowed us to produce, as Harry Rosenfeld, night foreign editor of the *Post,* later said, "the longest-running newspaper stories with the least amount of errors that I have ever experienced or will ever experience."

Reading 4: Watergate and the New Journalism

(10)   Watergate was a transforming event in the life of the *Washington Post*— as it was for many of us at the paper and throughout journalism. Anything as big as Watergate changes you, and I believe it changed not only the *Post* and me but journalism as a whole. There were both positive and negative effects.

(11)   In terms of positive effects, Watergate tested, for all of us at the *Post,* our whole organization: our talents, our skills, our ability to organize and mobilize resources to handle a long-term major investigation while still covering the daily news. In addition, ultimately Watergate showed what could be done by reporters relentlessly pursuing investigative work, by editors remaining as skeptical, demanding and dispassionate as possible under the circumstances, and by editorial writers helping to keep the questions foremost in the minds of our readers.

(12)   More important in terms of its effects, Watergate **propelled** the *Post* to true national and international prominence. The paper became known throughout the world because of it. On one level, the changed image of the *Post* was flattering; on another, it was both disturbing and distracting to getting on with other things. The positive press we began to get was heady and head-turning stuff, but the world, fortunately, has a way of keeping one humble. If the world didn't do it, I was determined to remind all of us of the need to keep arrogance under control.

(13)   Watergate also changed the way journalism and journalists are viewed, and in fact the way they work. During the Watergate affair, we—at the *Post* at least—had developed certain habits that were hard to break. John Anderson, an editorial writer, insightfully discussed this in some notes he made on the **editorial page** at the time:

"We had become used to a high degree of tension and drama. Morning editorial conferences were becoming almost frightful, as we went back and forth for hours over each day's events. Quickly they came to take up the entire morning, as we sat around with the papers spread out before us. The *Post*'s triumph in Watergate is well known, but we paid a large price for it which has had little attention. When it finally ended with Nixon's resignation, life for all of us was suddenly less interesting. For a long time afterwards news coverage was uneven and erratic because half the staff, particularly young reporters, were off chasing mini-scandals. It was a matter of years before we got back to consistent, orderly coverage of everyday news such as school boards and county council meetings."

(14)   Young people flocked into journalism, some for good reasons and some hoping to be Woodward and Bernstein. Certainly, Watergate provided a great deal of evidence that the national media do indeed shape events. Clearly, press reports contributed to **Judge John Sirica**'s doubts about what he was hearing in his courtroom, to congressional questions, and to public concern. But we didn't set out to have such a major impact. No one—least of all the press itself—thinks we are free from errors and faults or completely without bias. I never once have believed that we in the press do everything right, but we try to keep our opinions to the editorial page.

propelled: drove forward or onward
editorial page: a page in a newspaper where editors, publishers, or owners express their personal opinions about events in the news
Judge John Sirica: U.S. district court judge whose questioning of those involved in the 1972 Watergate break-in ultimately led to the resignation of President Richard Nixon

(15)   Also, the normal relationship between the press and the president, usually one of respectfully distant skepticism, was totally destroyed in the case
of Watergate, and that, too, affected journalism. I was somewhat alarmed
by certain tendencies toward over-involvement, which I felt we should over-
come as quickly as we could. The press after Watergate had to guard against
the romantic tendency to picture itself in the role of heroic champion of the
people, defending all virtues against the tyranny of the powerful. Watergate
had been a deviation from the normal, and I felt we couldn't look everywhere
for conspiracies and cover-ups. On the other hand, I don't believe we "over-
covered" Watergate, as some Nixon supporters claimed to the last.

(16)   As outstanding as Watergate was to the country and the government, it
underscored the role of a free, able, and energetic press. We saw how much
power the government has to reveal what it wants when it wants to give
people only the authorized version of events. We relearned the lessons of
the importance of the right of a newspaper to keep its sources confidential.

(17)   The credibility of the press stood the test of time against the credibility
of those who spent so much time self-righteously denying their own wrongdoing and assaulting us by questioning our performance and our motives.
In a speech I made in 1970—before Watergate—I said: "The cheap solu-
tions being sought by the administration will, in the long run, turn out to be
very costly." Indeed, they did.

Comprehension Check

Check your understanding of the reading selections by marking these
sentences true (*T*) or false (*F*).

___ 1. The Watergate scandal revolved around illegal activities surrounding the appointment of John Mitchell to President Nixon's cabinet.

___ 2. Watergate was the name of the building housing the national headquarters of the CRP, the Committee to Re-elect the President.

___ 3. The burglars who broke into the Watergate building were trying to
steal money kept at the Democratic National Headquarters.

___ 4. Initially, many *Post* readers wrote to Graham accusing her of unfair
journalistic practices.

__ 5. Bob Woodward and Carl Bernstein were the two main reporters covering the Watergate story for the *Post.*

__ 6. Initially, one of the things worrying Graham the most was that many other people in the media were intent on taking over, or appropriating, their story.

__ 7. One of the rigorous standards followed by the *Post* in reporting the story was to submit articles on Watergate to the White House press secretary.

__ 8. A negative effect of Watergate at the *Post* was that, after it was over, young reporters were more interested in making a name for themselves than in covering the everyday news.

Critical Thinking

Answer these questions by yourself. Then work with two or three other students to discuss the questions. Decide on a group answer to each question. Be prepared to explain your group's answers to the class.

1. What rigorous standards did the *Post* practice to make sure that Watergate reports were accurate?
2. What positive effects did covering the Watergate story have on the *Post*?
3. What negative effects did covering the story have on *Post* reporters?

Word Study

University Word List Vocabulary

comment

congress (congressional)

contribute

credible (credibility)

democracy (Democrats)

deviate (deviation)

execute (executive)

image

impact

investigate
  (investigation)

journal (journalism)

positive

role

ultimate (ultimately)

verify

Understanding Words

Word Parts

> ### Exercise 1: Prefixes

If you know that the prefix *inter-* means *between*, what would you expect to see in each of the following?

1. an *interracial* marriage

   _____

2. an *interfaith* religious service

   _____

3. an *interactive* video game

   _____

4. the *intervention* of a parent in an argument between two brothers

   _____

5. an *intersection* in the road

   _____

6. an *intergalactic* encounter in a science fiction movie

   _____

Exercise 2: Roots

The root *demo* from the Greek *demos,* meaning *people,* has given us the word *democracy* and its derivatives *democrat* and *democratic.* Keep that in mind while you answer the following questions by circling the letter of the correct answer.

1. Although of royal blood, the young prince has a very *democratic attitude* toward the crowds.

   Specifically, how do you expect the young prince to behave when he meets the crowd?

   I would expect him to
   a. smile, greet people warmly, and shake hands with some of them
   b. ignore them
   c. leave the area immediately

2. Historically, in the United States, the *Democratic Party* has been the party of the masses, of the common people.

   Which of the following segments of Americans do you think this party is likely to represent?
   a. landowners
   b. laborers
   c. businesspeople

3. Unlike Greece in its golden age, Americans have a *representative* rather than a *direct democracy.*

   How do you think a representative democracy works?
   a. Citizens express their views directly to the government.
   b. Only citizens with land and property are allowed to vote.
   c. All citizens elect legislators, such as senators or congresspeople, to speak for them.

4. Under *democracy* most Americans have enjoyed the right to vote, the right to bear arms, and the right to a free press.

   Which segment of the American people has always enjoyed these rights?
   a. Native Americans
   b. women
   c. white American men

5. In the American *democratic* system, injustices have historically been dealt with through legal changes to the Constitution.

   What are legal changes to the Constitution called?
   a. amendments
   b. executive orders
   c. judicial rulings

Word Relationships

Exercise 3: Synonyms

Cross out the word in each series that is not a synonym for the first word in that series. Use your dictionary if necessary.

1. credible	believable	plausible	unthinkable	acceptable
2. positive	doubtful	definite	categorical	certain
3. journal	diary	periodical	book	magazine
4. verify	document	validate	falsify	authenticate
5. deviate	conform	diverge	digress	depart
6. democracy	republic	monarchy	federation	commonwealth

Exercise 4: Synonyms

Although *reporter* and *commentator* are often entered in dictionaries as synonyms, these words do not have the exact same meaning.

A *reporter* is a person who provides the reader or listener with the news as it is happening. For example, if a tornado hits an area of the country, the reporter will give a basic account of the event: Where did it happen? When? How many people were killed or injured? How much damage has occurred?

A *commentator*, on the other hand, is someone who has the time to reflect on what is happening, to analyze particular events, fit them into other larger events, and relate them to broader issues and trends. After the tornado is over, a commentator might write or talk about the costs of providing federal help for tornado victims, the effect of this year's tornadoes on farm production, or the effectiveness of weather reports in preparing people for tornadoes.

Read the following journalistic events and indicate which of the following are likely to be covered by a reporter (*R*) and which by a commentator (*C*).

___ 1. an airplane crash
___ 2. possible reasons for the increasing number of air crashes over the past year
___ 3. an approaching hurricane
___ 4. an analysis of the influence of TV violence on real-life violent acts
___ 5. a raging forest fire

The Grammar of Words

Exercise 5: Derivatives

Complete the chart with derivatives of the italicized words. (Not all blanks can be filled in.)

Noun	Noun (person)	Adjective	Adverb	Verb
	executor		—	
democracy				
contribution				
		investigative	—	
		journalistic		
commentary, comment		—	—	
credibility	—			—

Exercise 6: Derivatives

Use the proper form of the word in parentheses to complete each sentence.

1. When writing a will it is customary to name an _____ (execute) to direct the distribution of assets.
2. One way to weaken a candidate's chance of winning is to ruin his or

   her _____ (credible).
3. The telescope is undoubtedly the most important _____ (investigate) tool in astronomy.
4. Who wrote the famous _____ (comment) on Aristotle's works?
5. Ordinary working people and laborers have traditionally voted for the

   _____ (democracy) Party.
6. Generally, Americans are great _____ (contribute) toward relief causes such as feeding hungry children or sending medical supplies to disaster areas.

Understanding Words in Sentences

Exercise 7: Reviewing Context Clues

A good strategy for finding out the meaning of a word is to use context clues. There are various types of context clues: synonym or brief definition, direct explanation, example, and contrast.

Circle the context clue that gives the meaning of the underlined word or phrase in the sentence. Identify the type of clue it is.

1. The best Graham could tell her reporters under the circumstances was to <u>investigate</u>, to look everywhere for hard evidence.

   Type of clue: _____
2. In the United States, <u>freedom of the press</u> is one of the basic rights protected by the Constitution. That is, newspapers, magazines, radio, and television are at liberty to disclose any story about events or people.

   Type of clue: _____

3. This unit is about <u>journalism,</u> the field of producing, gathering, and reporting news for the media.

   Type of clue: _____

4. In the main, campaign tactics are considered fair game as long as they are legal, as long as they don't break any laws. Watergate, however, revolved around a wide range of <u>illegal</u> activities undertaken by high-ranking Republicans to secure the reelection of President Nixon in 1972.

   Type of clue: _____

5. Peter said, "I hope you are using <u>rigorous journalistic standards.</u>" Indeed, we were. We always did our best to be careful and responsible. From the beginning, the editors had made up their minds to handle the story with more than the usual exacting, precise attention to fairness and detail.

   Type of clue: _____

6. More important in terms of its effects, Watergate propelled the *Post* to true national and <u>international prominence.</u> The paper became known throughout the world because of it.

   Type of clue: _____

Exercise 8: Word Meanings in Context

Read the following sentences. Then complete the sentences by circling the letter of the correct choice.

1. The three major <u>networks</u> carried the president's State of the Union message.

   In this case, *networks* are
   a. chains of radio and television stations
   b. personal connections that can provide assistance in a particular business or endeavor
   c. a system of connected elements, such as lines, channels, or computers

2. There are excellent support <u>networks</u> for people who have experienced a great loss.

   In this case, *networks* are
   a. chains of radio and television stations
   b. personal connections that can provide assistance in a particular business or endeavor
   c. a system of connected elements, such as lines, channels, or computers

3. He was absolutely <u>positive</u> that the blond man was the person who had robbed the store.

   In this case, *positive* means
   a. a number greater than zero
   b. certain
   c. having a good effect

4. One <u>positive</u> outcome of the treatment was that she was in better overall health.

   In this case, *positive* means
   a. a number greater than zero
   b. certain
   c. having a good effect

5. Many consider Michelangelo's *David* to be the <u>image</u> of the perfect man.

   In this case, *image* means
   a. the likeness or imitation of something
   b. a mental representation or idea
   c. a visual picture, like a face in a mirror

6. His <u>image</u> of heaven is that it is the place where God lives.

   In this case, *image* means
   a. the likeness or imitation of something
   b. a mental representation or idea
   c. a visual picture, like a face in a mirror

Exercise 9: Identifying People

Scan the Reading Preview and reading passages to find the sentence that identifies the job of each of these people. Write the person's job on the line provided. Also write "Reading Preview" or the number of the reading paragraph to indicate where you found the information.

1. John Dean _____

2. John Mitchell _____

3. H. R. Haldeman _____

4. Archibald Cox _____

5. Peter Peterson _____

6. John Sirica _____

Using Words in Communication

Exercise 10: Listening

There is a question before each listening text. As you listen to the text, focus on getting the answer to this question.

1. Question: What was the money in the secret fund to be used for?

   Answer: _____
2. Question: What had Woodward found out about H. R. Haldeman from his secret source?

   Answer: _____
3. Question: Who did Nixon ask to conduct an investigation of a possible White House connection to the burglary?

   Answer: _____
4. Question: What were Nixon people not to accept invitations for?

   Answer: _____

5. Question: How did President Nixon transmit his directive to his chief of staff?

   Answer: _____

6. Question: Besides a newspaper, what other journalistic media did the Post Company own?

   Answer: _____

Exercise 11: Speaking

Skim the reading selection to find the context in which these idioms appear. Work with two or three classmates and discuss what you think the idioms mean.

1. They didn't jump on it.   Paragraph __

   Meaning: _____

2. We did not want to be set up.   Paragraph __

   Meaning: _____

3. We paid a large price.   Paragraph __

   Meaning: _____

4. It stood the test of time.   Paragraph __

   Meaning: _____

Exercise 12: Speaking

Go back to the first reading passage and reread the descriptions of the two Watergate scandal reporters: Bob Woodward and Carl Bernstein. Then, in small groups, discuss your answers to the following questions.

1. According to Katharine Graham, which personal traits or attributes make Bob Woodward an effective reporter?
2. According to Katharine Graham, which personal traits or characteristics almost stopped Carl Bernstein from working on the Watergate story?

Exercise 13: Reading

Research the political career of John Mitchell using the internet or library resources. Develop a time line showing the highlights of his career until he was sentenced for his involvement in the Watergate scandal.

Exercise 14: Writing

Write a paragraph comparing and contrasting Bob Woodward with Carl Bernstein. You may want to watch the movie *All the President's Men* and compare and contrast the portrayals in the movie with Graham's descriptions.

Unit 5
María Martínez

Vocabulary Preview

Preview 1

Complete each sentence with the most suitable word.

diverse   fragments   carbonize   indigenous   aligned

1. Piles of split wood are neatly _____ beside the fire.

2. Dr. Hewett suggested that they use only _____ designs from the ruins where their Tewa ancestors had lived.

3. The excavations turned up _____ of a kind of pottery not previously found in the Southwest.

4. Even without a potter's wheel, _____ New World cultures and civilizations have produced some of the world's most beautiful pottery.

5. Black-on-black pottery is made by smothering the fire with manure to

   _____ the clay black.

Preview 2

Look at the way the underlined words are used in the sentences. Match each word with its definition.

1. Logically, he knew it was the best job offer he would receive; intuitively, though, he knew he wouldn't be happy working there.

2. There's a distinct possibility that, because of bad weather, all flights will be canceled this morning.

3. At holiday time, many people prefer to stay away from stores and do their shopping through mail-order catalogs.

4. Anthropology is the science that deals with the origins, development, and cultural practices of humans.

5. The circulatory system is the system that distributes blood throughout the body.

___ 1. intuitive
___ 2. distinct
___ 3. catalog
___ 4. anthropology
___ 5. circulate

a. clear; likely
b. to move in a circle or circuit
c. the study of cultures
d. insightful; without using reason
e. a booklet containing a list of items

Reading Preview: What Do You Know about María Martínez?

Work with two or three other students and draw up a list of the names, places, and things you associate with the following topics.

1. Who are the Native Americans? Where do they live? What do you know about their present way of life?
2. María and her family lived in a pueblo in the American Southwest. Where is the American Southwest? What characterizes a pueblo?
3. María was a potter. What do you know about pottery making? What are the two most common ways of making pottery? What is a kiln?

Adapted from *The Living Tradition of María Martínez* by Susan Peterson (New York: Kodansha International, 1977), 89–94, 215–20.

Introduction to the Readings

María Martínez, the great **Tewa** potter, is best known for the beautifully **burnished** black-on-black pottery that she perfected with her husband, Julian, in the second decade of this century. The distinctive characteristic of this magnificent pottery, prized by collectors and museums throughout North America and Europe, is that although **unglazed,** it glows with a brilliant **sheen.** What follow are two adapted excerpts from Susan Peterson's *The Living Tradition of María Martínez:* "Black-on-Black Pottery," which tells how this particular type of pottery came to be made, and "The Firing," a description of a crucial aspect of making the pottery.

Reading 1: Black-on-Black Pottery

(1)   María speaks often of the **excavations** conducted by a group of archaeologists in 1908 and 1909. They were led by Dr. Edgar Lee Hewett, a professor of **archaeology** and Director of the Museum of New Mexico, who had been commissioned to research ruined pueblos of the Tewa. This work resulted in findings of exceptional interest. Hewett's excavation, one of several conducted in the **ruins** around **San Ildefonso** for a period of years, turned up fragments of a kind of pottery not previously found in the Southwest. These **shards** were jet and charcoal black in color, and some of them were polished.

Tewa: an Indian tribe of the American Southwest
burnished: glistening; polished to a brilliant shine
unglazed: dull; without any finish coating
sheen: shine; luster; polish
excavations: digs designed to expose the ruins of ancient civilizations
archaeology: the study of the life of ancient peoples, often done by investigating sites or ruins
ruins: what is left of something (such as a city, building, or structure) that once existed
San Ildefonso: the name of a communal village in the Southwestern United States made up of typical terraced adobe dwellings
shards: fragments; pieces of pottery

They were quite different from the characteristic black-on-red or black-on-cream wares of the type commonly found in the district.

(2)   Hewett was especially impressed with the black shards. He wanted to find an Indian potter in the vicinity and was given the name of María Martínez as one who could make the thinnest, roundest pots in the least time. He visited her at the pueblo with some of the unusual shards and asked her to make pots the way she thought these pieces would have looked when they were whole. María accepted the challenge. This was the beginning of the now famous black pottery of San Ildefonso that María and her family have developed and perfected for more than half a century.

(3)   Originally, María and Julian's black pots had no decoration and were only for Dr. Hewett's experiments. It was not until 1918 that the first decorated black ware, painted by Julian, was made and **fired.** Two black pots that supposedly are from this first firing are now in the collection of the Museum of New Mexico's Laboratory of Anthropology at Santa Fe. María says that it was very difficult, at first, to burnish a design while leaving the rest of the background unpolished. But she and Julian kept experimenting and, after a few more firings, they achieved the desired effect by reversing the background and the designs. The first treatment had consisted of using **matte background** surfaces for highly polished designs. Later ones consisted of polishing the whole background first and, then, printing on the matte decoration. This is the style famous today.

(4)   The Indian people of both North and South America never developed the potter's wheel. Yet the diverse New World cultures and civilizations have produced some of the world's most beautiful and refined pottery. Even today the Indian potter prefers to **coil** rather than **throw a pot.**

(5)   This was the case with María, too. As she struggled to develop her craft, she tried to make larger pots and to achieve greater **symmetry** but only by coiling the clay. To make thin-walled pots of perfect symmetry by coiling alone is a major accomplishment. It is extremely arduous to work with the difficult clay María used. No modern studio potter, with access to supply house catalogs, would dream of working with such stuff. Yet María coiled monumental pots with this material.

(6)   Eventually, María perfected her burnishing technique so that the surface

fired: baked in a kiln
matte background: a dull surface finish; not shiny
coil: to wind clay into rings, one above the other
throw a pot: to shape a pot using a potter's wheel
symmetry: When something has symmetry, its two sides are exactly the same.

was absolutely unblemished, with no strokes showing. She and Julian kept experimenting with the firing to get the most intense black and the highest shine. And Julian continued to decorate. Dr. Hewett suggested he and María use only indigenous designs from the ruins where their Tewa ancestors had lived and they accepted the suggestion. They built their forms and decoration on the basis of the art of their own people. Some of the old stylized patterns are thought to be mountains, clouds, and mythical symbols such as the water serpent. The black-on-black ware, as it was eventually called, was made by painting designs on after the pot was polished and then **smothering** the fire with manure to carbonize the clay black. But it was the silvery black color, with or without the matte patterns on the pots, that brought the worldwide distinction the Martínez family enjoys today.

Reading 2: The Firing

(7)   It is important to begin early, when there is no wind. We walk to the **firing shed,** a place hidden from view. The area is open except for a few trees behind the shed. Everyone comes to the shed carrying pots, and more pots will be brought in the truck. The shed is made of weathered boards; one side is open. Along one inside wall dry

cow chips are neatly piled three feet high, two feet deep, and covered by a wooden board. It is an amazing collection—**cow paddies** stacked like so many flat cheeses.

(8)   A square iron grill, placed in the center of the shed, is held off the dirt by **charred** 46-ounce tomato cans eight inches high. A pile of wood ash is

smothering: covering a fire with something to put it out or lower the flame
firing shed: a small outbuilding where pottery is baked or fired
cow chips or paddies: The solid excrement or waste of cows that is shaped into rounds or ovals before it dries. These may be burned instead of wood in fires.
charred: partly burned and blackened by fire

on the ground. Piles of split wood are neatly aligned, and there are two wash-tubs full of horse **manure** which has been worked into a very fine texture.

(9)   The potters laugh and talk quietly as they work together. They are establishing the position of the grill and the wood underneath. Sometimes one of them takes a great deal of time locating a stick, perhaps repositioning it several times. Then one of the others will come along and move it elsewhere, taking the same time again in placement.

(10)   The basic iron grill is made of horizontal bars. Another old rectangular grate, a large iron square, is set over this. Next, iron burner plates from old gas stoves and older heavy **perforated** metal grills are laid over those, making a delightful grid pattern of highlights and shadows in the sun. When this is accomplished after considerable time and much care, the potters take positions on each side of the "**kiln**" and begin the next step. Thin, long strips of tin are placed exactly, side by side, overlapping, until there are no open spaces and no fire can touch the pots from beneath.

(11)   The wood is then set under the grill, in three layers. These pieces are about two feet long by several inches square. Layers crisscross each other and are arranged to extend slightly outside the grill area. The manner in which the wood is distributed under the grill, and the quantity of it, will determine the initial impact and heat of the fire.

(12)   Next **twigs** are sprinkled over the logs—three or four handfuls. Pots are brought in their baskets and trays, taken out and set on the ground. The potters walk around assessing the ware, planning how to stack it on the grill, but not speaking. They work intuitively, in complete harmony, without needing words or directions.

(13)   Each one chooses a pot. Holding it with spread fingertips or balancing it from the inside, gingerly protecting the polish, each person places his piece carefully upside down on the grill, not in the shadow of another and never touching. The attempt is to balance the vessel properly the first time. Movement may knock or crack the fragile ware or fingerprint the burnish, but some rearranging is always necessary. The pots will be piled checkerboard fashion three high, not more. Metal canning jar lids, burned and charred from previous fires, are used to steady smaller shapes. The pots glisten brick-red in the sun; it is hard to imagine that they will be black after the firing.

manure: animal excrement that is used to fertilize fields
perforated: having holes pierced through the surface
kiln: an oven in which pottery or bricks are baked
twigs: small, thin branches of trees or bushes

(14)   Everyone is intent. No one speaks. Two of the potters bend over to select pots from the ground and bend again over the grill, holding body and
arms steady as they work to position each piece **a hair's distance** from the
next. Plates are laid last, on the top layer. They are held lightly but surely
with spread fingers and set upside down over the seemingly unsteady pile of
pottery. Only the smallest pinpoint of edge touches another shape so that
all surfaces are free to be affected evenly by the firing atmosphere.

(15)   One of the potters leans over and tosses more twigs under the grill on
top of the logs. Then he sprinkles kerosene over the wood so when it is lit,
a strong fire will spring up quickly and evenly with tall flames. There are many
ways of starting the fire, but the pueblo way is to quickly ignite the open fire
around the pots by pouring kerosene onto the wood, so that the heat is im-
mediate and even. Very few clays in the world can stand the treatment without exploding. No wonder the Indians treasure their rare clay deposit.

(16)   Next **army mess trays** and old **license plates,** blackened from many firings, are set vertically around the grate to form a shield, leaving an opening
at each corner of the square and also two openings in the center of each of
the four sides for **draft.**

(17)   Of course, this structure of tin-can-supported iron grill that constitutes
an oven for pots, shielded by metal plates and cow dung, is a far cry from the
type of kiln used by most contemporary potters. On the other hand, the principles involved in building this rudimentary "kiln" are basically the same as
those of modern firing chambers. Wood as fuel is not as common today as
gas or oil or electricity, but it is used by stoneware and porcelain potters.

(18)   An open-fire kiln such as María's family constructs has a great deal of
precedent through the ages of man. Whether in a hole in the ground lined
with clay or with pieces of fired pottery, or a simple pile of pots covered with
stones and with only twigs for a fire, or a cave in a hillside, an open fire has
been used for hardening clay vessels since the beginning of the craft. María
and her family have improved the ancient method by adding the metal **insulation** and by raising the grill off the ground so that the fire has better circulation and the pots a more even atmosphere.

(19)   The last step in preparation for the fire is to lay the outside dung wall,
which will form the insulation for the heat treatment. Two of the potters choose

a hair's distance: very, very close
army mess trays: the metal trays soldiers use in their mess hall (cafeteria) to get their food
license plates: metal plates that drivers must attach to a car in order to show that the car is registered
draft: a current of air moving through an area
insulation: protective material used to prevent escape of heat, cold, and so on

large round cow chips from the storage place at the side of the shed and stand them on edge against the metal. They begin with the largest ones first and then smaller ones to fill in. More chips are laid across the top, and the "kiln" is finished. The potters stand back to observe the "kiln" they have made. They nod in approval. It's time to light the fire.

Comprehension Check

Check your understanding of the reading selections by marking these sentences true (*T*) or false (*F*).

__ 1. The first reading explains the origin of black-on-black pottery. The second reading tells how the pots are fired.

__ 2. Dr. Hewett and his team found fragments of a kind of pottery that had not been found previously in excavations in the Southwest.

__ 3. María and her family were from a pueblo called Santa Clara.

__ 4. The Tewa Indians of the Southwest developed the potter's wheel.

__ 5. A characteristic of black-on-black pottery is that it is totally smooth, without decorations.

__ 6. The best time to fire pottery is in the evening, when there is no wind.

__ 7. The basic grill for firing black-on-black pottery is made of split wood.

__ 8. The initial impact and heat of the fire are determined by the quantity of wood used and the way in which the wood is distributed under the grill.

Critical Thinking

First respond to item 1. Then work with two or three other students to discuss questions 2 and 3. Decide on a group answer to each question. Be prepared to explain your group answers to the class.

1. In your own words, tell another student how Dr. Hewett's excavations led to the making of black-on-black pottery.

2. Why are the potters quiet when they prepare for a firing? What would some of the advantages and disadvantages of this be?
3. According to the readings, what are some of the differences between traditional Tewa and modern pottery making methods? What are some of the similarities between the two methods?

Word Study

 University Word List Vocabulary

align	diverse	locate
anthropology	eventual (eventually)	myth (mythical)
carbon (carbonize)	fragment	precede (precedent)
catalog	fuel	style (stylized)
circulate (circulation)	indigenous	technique
distinct (distinction)	intuitive (intuitively)	vertical (vertically)

Understanding Words

Word Parts

Exercise 1: Prefixes

The prefix *pre-*, from the Latin *prae*, means *before*. Match the words with their definitions. Use your dicitionary if necessary.

___ 1. preliminary
___ 2. premature
___ 3. presuppose
___ 4. precede
___ 5. precedent
___ 6. prevent

a. to assume beforehand
b. a statement or an act that may serve as justifi-
   cation for a later one
c. arriving before the expected time
d. before or leading to the main action
e. to come before
f. to stop from doing or happening

Exercise 2: Prefixes

Complete the following sentences by using one of the words in Exercise 1. Add word endings if necessary.

1. Crushed stone may be used to _____ the wind and rain from causing soil erosion.

2. A _____, in law, is a judgment or decision that is cited to jus-tify deciding a similar case in the same manner.

3. Middle age is the period of human adulthood that _____ old age.

4. His advanced text in mathematics _____ knowledge about how to add, subtract, multiply, and divide.

5. A _____ hearing is one in which the judge decides whether or not there is sufficient evidence to justify proceeding with a case.

6. A _____ birth is any birth that occurs significantly before the expected date of delivery.

Word Relationships

Exercise 3: Synonyms

Write three words that are synonyms for each of the words given.

1. style   _____   _____   _____

2. myth   _____   _____   _____

3. diverse   _____   _____   _____

4. distinct   _____   _____   _____

5. technique   _____   _____   _____

6. intuitive   _____   _____   _____

Exercise 4: Antonyms

Write the word from this unit that fits each definition. Add a word ending if necessary. Then provide an antonym for that word.

Definition	Word	Antonym
1. standing or pointing straight up	_____	_____
2. to come before	_____	_____
3. ultimately happening	_____	_____
4. broken pieces	_____	_____
5. originally from a particular area	_____	_____
6. knowing without thinking	_____	_____

The Grammar of Words

Exercise 5: Changing Adjectives to Adverbs

Adjectives with the suffix *-al*, meaning *related to,* are commonly changed into adverbs by adding *-ly. Example: initial + -ly = initially.*

Change these adjectives to adverbs.

Adjective	*Adverb*
1. original	_____
2. usual	_____
3. eventual	_____
4. habitual	_____
5. ultimate	_____
6. final	_____

Exercise 6: Using Adjectives and Adverbs

Adjectives modify nouns; adverbs modify verbs, adjectives, or adverbs. Which word is each underlined word modifying? Classify this word as a noun (N), a verb (V), an adjective (Adj), or an adverb (Adv).

1. A barre is a horizontal handrail, <u>usually</u> wooden, that dancers use for their warm-up exercises.
2. A <u>habitual</u> offender is a criminal who has been frequently caught and convicted.
3. Nankeen is a durable cotton cloth that was <u>originally</u> made in China but is now imitated in many other countries.
4. In *Macbeth*, Malcolm, son of Duncan, is <u>eventually</u> named king of Scotland.
5. He disagrees with his father now, but <u>ultimately</u> he will understand his father's point of view.
6. William Penn's <u>final</u> years were very unhappy.

Word Being Modified	*Classification*
1. _____	_____
2. _____	_____
3. _____	_____
4. _____	_____
5. _____	_____
6. _____	_____

Word Meanings

Exercise 7: Synonyms for *Myth*

Although *fable, parable, legend, allegory,* and *epic* are often given as synonyms for the word *myth,* they are similar only in that each of these *tells a story.* Each synonym, though, means to tell a *particular kind* of story. Do you know which synonym is most appropriate for each of the following stories?

__ 1. fable

__ 2. parable

__ 3. legend

__ 4. allegory

__ 5. epic

a. A short, fictitious story of the kind used by Jesus in preaching to his audience. "The Prodigal Son" is an example of this type of story.

b. A moral story in which animals speak and act like humans. "The Tortoise and the Hare" is an example of this type of story.

c. A story in which symbolic figures with names such as Truth and Everyman are used to generalize about human experience. "The Cave" is an example of this type of story.

d. A long narrative poem that relates the deeds of a hero. *Beowulf* is an example of this type of story.

e. A story, such as "King Arthur and the Knights of the Round Table," that is often regarded as historical but, in fact, is not verifiable.

Understanding Words in Sentences

Exercise 8: Word Meanings in Context

Read the text that follows. Then work with two or three other students to fill in the blanks with one of the words given in the list. Finally, answer the questions on your own.

black	compounds	element	jewels
carbon	conductor	fuel	organisms
chemistry	diamond	graphite	paper
coal	electricity	hardness	soft

Learning about Carbon

(1)   _____, a nonmetallic chemical _____, exists in three

forms. Two of the forms are _____ and _____. Pure diamond is the hardest naturally occurring substance known and is a poor

_____ of electricity. Graphite, on the other hand, is a _____, slippery solid that is a good conductor of both heat and _____.

Because of their beauty, diamonds are valued as _____, and because of their _____, they are valued for cutting, grinding, and drilling.

(2)   The third form of carbon, known as carbon black, is amorphous, meaning that it lacks a definite form. Included in carbon black are charcoal, coke,

and _____. All forms of carbon _____ are products of oxidation, that is, of uniting with oxygen. Oxidation occurs in burning or rusting and in other forms of decomposition of organic compounds. Carbon black has many uses. In addition to being used extensively as

_____, it is also used to make ink, typewriter ribbons, and carbon

_____.

(3)   Carbon combines and links easily with other atoms to form over a million carbon _____. In fact, carbon's compounds are so numerous, complex, and important that their study constitutes a specialized field of chemistry called organic _____. The field of organic chemistry derives its name from the fact that, in the nineteenth century, most of the then-known carbon compounds were considered to have originated in living _____.

Questions

1. What are the three forms of carbon given in the reading?
2. Give two reasons diamonds are valued.
3. Explain how organic chemistry got its name.

Exercise 9: Word Meanings in Context

In the reading passages, scan for the words given in the following list. The number of the paragraph containing the word is given in parentheses. Circle the letter of the meaning that is most appropriate within the context of the reading passage.

1. catalogs (5)
   a. makes an alphabetized list
   b. brochures displaying items for sale
   c. pictures

2. stylized (6)
   a. shaped by a hairdresser
   b. beautifully written
   c. artistically, rather than naturally, fashioned

3. distinction (6)
   a. reputation
   b. clear vision
   c. difference

4. aligned (8)
   a. cleaned up
   b. adjusted
   c. lined up

5. locating (9)
   a. finding
   b. positioning
   c. stumbling on

Exercise 10: Using Words Correctly

The most common meanings of *circulate* are

a. to move around in a circle or an orbit
b. to go from group to group at a social gathering
c. to be sold or distributed
d. to become well known

Look at the way the word *circulate* is used in the following sentences. For each sentence write the letter of the meaning that best fits in that context.

___ 1. "Don't just sit there," she said. "<u>Circulate</u> around the room and give people a chance to see how interesting you are."
___ 2. When lumber is "seasoned," the wood is cut into boards and stacked so that the air can <u>circulate</u> freely around each piece.
___ 3. A blood vessel is a tiny tube inside the body through which blood <u>circulates.</u>
___ 4. Many early civilizations manufactured products, such as pottery and oils, that <u>circulated</u> along the trade routes.
___ 5. Rumors of the disastrous financial report <u>circulated</u> through Wall Street.
___ 6. The two-dollar bill is rarely seen in <u>circulation.</u>
___ 7. Old-fashioned radiators, <u>circulating</u> steam through pipes, were used to heat the house.
___ 8. At the end of the news conference, she <u>circulated</u> around the room hoping to find a journalist who was willing to write about her experience.

Using Words in Communication

Exercise 11: Listening

Listen to the texts on the audiotape until you understand them. Then circle the correct answers.

1. In making a piece of traditional black ware pottery, what step precedes forming the sides of the pot?
   a. adding coils of clay
   b. pounding the clay by hand into a pancake shape
   c. firing the pot

2. How are the coils of clay held together?
   a. by wetting them
   b. by pounding them
   c. by pinching them

3. What tool do traditional potters like to use in forming their pots?
   a. gourds
   b. tongue depressors
   c. spatulas

4. In order to finish their pots properly, how do Tewa potters need to keep their tools?
   a. softened
   b. hard
   c. wet

5. What had Tewa potters of past generations used to smooth the surface of their pots?
   a. kernels of corn
   b. dekerneled corncobs
   c. sandpaper

Exercise 12: Speaking

Reread the reading passages to find the answers to the following questions. Then, with another student, take turns asking and answering the questions.

1. What is María Martínez known for?
2. Where did Dr. Hewett and his team find unusual shards of pottery?
3. Generally, in what stage of pottery making was Julian most involved?
4. How did María and Julian finally achieve the desired effect with their pots?

5. What mythical Tewa symbols are reflected in María's pottery?
6. How are newly made pots taken to the firing shed?
7. How is the square iron grill held up?
8. Where in the United States is San Ildefonso pueblo located?

Exericise 13: Writing

Research one of the following topics using books, journals, magazines, and the Internet. Summarize the information you find on 4″ × 6″ index cards. Turn the cards in to your teacher.

1. The art of pottery making
2. Margaret Tafoya (or any other traditional potter of the Southwest)
3. San Ildefonso (or any of the other pueblos of the American Southwest)
4. Pottery making in my own country
5. Famous potters of . . . (any country in the world)

Exercise 14: Oral Presentation

Using the cards you prepare for Exercise 13, give a three- to four-minute presentation about your topic to a group of classmates. Then ask the group at least two questions about your topic.

Exercise 15: Reading

Read each text and the questions that follow it. Then provide the meaning of the underlined words in the questions as used in this context. Finally, answer the questions.

Pueblo Indian Culture

Many centuries before European explorers found their way to the Western Hemisphere, the Pueblo Indians of what is now New Mexico developed a distinctive civilization. These peace-loving people created an urban life that was in harmony with the environment, and they also lived in harmony with each other. Their religion was deeply spiritual and constituted an important part of their daily life within which they created highly developed art, especially in pottery, weaving, jewelry, textiles, and leatherwork.

From information provided by the Pueblo Cultural Center, Albuquerque, New Mexico.

Today, after suffering disruption by the American westward expansion, the Pueblo people are settled in nineteen communities, some of which have been continuously inhabited since long before the discovery of America. Still retaining their ancient and largely secret ceremonial life, they nevertheless welcome visitors from all over the world and offer a glimpse of the proud heritage that they have kept alive for more than a thousand years.

One of the best known pueblos of New Mexico is San Ildefonso. It is renowned for the famous black-on-black pottery that originated there. In the 1920s, Native American crafts began to be popular with collectors. This proved to be fortunate for the San Ildefonso people because a number of artisans in the community set to work and were able to improve the economic conditions of the pueblo. Before long the outstanding quality of San Ildefonso pottery became known. It was then that the famous black pots were revived, primarily because of María Martínez. Today these pots command worldwide the respect of collectors of fine art.

Questions

1. What <u>anthropological</u> information about the Pueblo Indians appears in this text?

2. What is San Ildefonso? What is <u>distinctive</u> about it?

3. According to this text, who <u>preceded</u> Europeans on the American continent?

The Making of Traditional Tewa Pottery

Traditional Tewa pottery making must satisfy the following requirements:

a. The article must be formed with raw materials available from tribal lands. These materials should be purified manually, preferably by the potter or close members of the potter's family.

From Mary Ellen Blair and Lawrence Blair, *Margaret Tafoya: A Tewa Potter's Heritage and Legacy* (Westchester, PA: Schiffer, 1986, 88).

b. The ware must be formed and finished by hand methods such as coiling or pinching. These methods have their roots in the prehistoric or historic Tewa past. The use of the potter's wheel or plaster molds is frowned upon by the classic Tewa potter.

c. The work must be fired in temporary kilns built on the spot at the time of each individual firing, using only wood or manure as fuel. Firing in commercially available kilns, heated with secondary fuel such as oil, or electricity, is considered an especially poor practice.

Questions

1. What is <u>distinctive</u> about the way materials are used in Tewa pottery making?

2. What are the traditional requirements of this <u>technique?</u>

3. What are the traditional requirements regarding the kind of <u>fuel</u> used in the firing?

Unit 6
Madeleine Albright

Vocabulary Preview

Preview 1

Complete each sentence with the most suitable word.

academically   affluent   constantly   frustrated   linguist

1. Mr. Korbel loved to walk, and he was _____ when people driving by stopped to ask him if he wanted a ride.

2. Madeleine was an accomplished _____. She spoke Czech, French, and English fluently by the time she was eleven.

3. In Czechoslovakia, the Korbel family had been relatively

   _____. They had lived in luxurious homes and had servants to help with the cooking and cleaning.

4. Mrs. Korbel loved to watch soap operas. She listened to them

   _____, hoping to hear how the story would end.

5. Madeleine was _____ qualified to go into the seventh grade, but, because she was only eleven, she was put into the sixth grade instead.

Preview 2

Look at the way the underlined words are used in the sentences. Match each word with its definition.

1. She didn't speak Spanish well, but her French was very <u>fluent.</u> Everyone thought she was French.
2. Individual committees will meet in the morning, and the entire group will <u>convene</u> after lunch for a general meeting.
3. Every summer, tourists <u>invade</u> the quiet seaside town—the roads are blocked by traffic jams, and the beaches are filled with people.
4. The term "marital <u>status</u>" refers to whether a person is married, single, divorced, or widowed.
5. In many countries, driving while drunk is a serious <u>violation</u> of the law.

___ 1. fluent   a. to come together; to assemble
___ 2. convene   b. a person's position in society
___ 3. invade   c. the breaking of rules or laws
___ 4. status   d. able to speak a language easily and well
___ 5. violation   e. to occupy; to overrun; to attack

Reading Preview: What Do You Know about Madeleine Albright?

Circle the correct answer. If you don't know the answer, guess.

1. Madeleine Albright
    a. is the president of Wellesley College
    b. received the Nobel Peace Prize for her work on human rights
    c. was the first woman to be appointed U.S. secretary of state
    d. is currently living in Czechoslovakia

2. Madeleine Albright
    a. was the daughter of a Czechoslovakian diplomat
    b. spent some of her childhood years in England and Switzerland
    c. immigrated to the United States at the age of eleven
    d. all of the above

3. Which of the following did not contribute to Madeleine Albright's appointment as secretary of state?
    a. Madeleine graduated from Wellesley College.
    b. Clinton trusted her judgment and liked the way she expressed her opinions.
    c. Women's groups wanted him to appoint a woman to a cabinet position.
    d. Madeleine spoke several languages fluently.

Adapted from *Seasons of Her Life: A Biography of Madeleine Korbel Albright* by Ann Blackman (New York: Lisa Drew Book/Scribner, 1998), 84–85, 93–95, 250–52, 256–57.

Introduction to the Readings

Madeleine Albright is the first woman to ever hold the position of U.S. **secretary of state;** as secretary of state she is the highest-ranking woman in the U.S. government. President Bill Clinton, the forty-second president of the United States, nominated Albright for the position on December 5, 1996, and she was sworn in as sixty-fourth secretary of state on January 23, 1997. Prior to her appointment as secretary of state, Albright served as the U.S. representative to the United Nations and as a member of President Clinton's cabinet and the National Security Council. During her tenure as secretary of state, Albright has had to deal with difficult political problems in many parts of the world: the Balkans, the Middle East, Iraq, Africa, and Ireland, to name just a few.

Madeleine Albright has been involved in international affairs since childhood. One might say she was born into them. Her father, Josef Korbel, was a diplomat in her native country of Czechoslovakia. The events of World War II, however, made it dangerous for the Korbel family to stay in Europe. The family moved to England and then later immigrated to the United States in 1948. This background probably helped Albright become an accomplished linguist. Today, besides speaking English as if it were her first language, Albright also speaks French and Czech fluently and has good reading and speaking abilities in Russian and Polish.

The readings here, adapted from *Seasons of Her Life* by Ann Blackman, tell about two periods in Madeleine's life: moving to the United States as a child and the years just prior to her appointment as secretary of state.

Reading 1: Starting Over

(1)   On the evening of November 5, 1948, Mandula Korbel and her three children—Madeleine, Kathy and John—boarded the ship the SS *America* in Southhampton, England. They carried twenty-one pieces of luggage. As the family of a diplomat they traveled first class. The ship sailed overnight across the English Channel to the port city of Le Havre. When the passengers woke up in the morning, the port was calm. But the minute the ship set sail again, winter weather set in. The ocean turned wild. Mandula was seasick for almost

secretary of state: The secretary of state is appointed by the President of the United States and confirmed by the Senate. One of the secretary's duties is to serve as the President's chief foreign affairs adviser.

the entire six-day trip. She remained in her **cabin** while Madeleine cared for Kathy and John. On November 11, **Armistice Day,** the ship arrived in New York. The Korbels stood on the ship's deck as they sailed past the Statue of Liberty. Just ten days before, Madeleine and her family had listened to American election returns on the radio and cheered when **Harry S. Truman** won an extraordinary, last-minute victory over New York governor Thomas E. Dewey. Truman would be her new country's president. This was the beginning of Madeleine Korbel's political awareness. She was eleven years old.

(2)   Madeleine's father, Josef Korbel, arrived in New York on December 22, 1948. Soon after that the family settled into a home just outside New York City in Great Neck, a prosperous and developing suburban community on Long Island's north shore. In Czechoslovakia, the Korbels had been a relatively affluent family. As diplomats, they had lived in comfortable, sometimes luxurious quarters and had help to take care of the daily cooking and cleaning. In Great Neck, Mandula kept house herself. "Mother used to tell stories of how she had to buy pots and pans, but didn't know what to choose because she had never cooked. She had no idea of what foods to buy or in what quantity," says John Korbel. "We started a completely new life in 1949."

(3)   Mr. Korbel chose the area because the United Nations' temporary headquarters was located in Lake Success, one of the seven villages of Great Neck. Korbel loved to walk the town's country roads, but it frustrated him that every few minutes, someone stopped to ask if he wanted a ride. "People in America are not used to walking," he told his family.

(4)   Madeleine and Kathy went to an elementary school about a mile from their house. The school had a big playground and across the street was a shop where the children sometimes bought hot dogs for lunch. The Korbels did not have television, so Madeleine watched children's TV shows at the home of a neighbor. Mandula Korbel later discovered soap operas. She listened constantly for the end of the story, which never seemed to come.

(5)   At eleven, Madeleine was a pretty girl, slightly round with soft blond curls and a wide, friendly smile. Like her father, she was already an accomplished linguist, fluent in three languages: Czech, which she would use at home with her parents; French, which she had first learned at a boarding school in Switzerland; and English, which she spoke with a British accent. Although Madeleine was the appropriate age for sixth grade, initially school officials thought she should go into fifth grade because she was a foreigner and un-

cabin: a private room used for living and sleeping on a ship or boat
Armistice Day: the day celebrating the end of World War I, November 11, 1918
Harry S. Truman: The thirty-third President of the United States. Truman held this position from 1945 to 1953.

familiar with American ways. But when they tested her, they found that academically she qualified for seventh grade. Taking into account the discrete issues of her age, background, and test scores, the officials decided to place her in sixth grade.

(6)   At first, Madeleine did not realize that she spoke differently from the other children. One day in school, her class was learning a song and Madeleine heard one voice that did not blend in. Listening carefully, she recognized the voice was her own. That was the first time she realized she had a British accent, and she was determined to lose it. Not only did Madeleine sound different from other children, but she looked different as well, her coats a little too big or a little too small, dresses a little too short or a little too long—never quite right. Her schoolmates had the occasional parties of early **adolescence,** but Madeleine rarely went. Her parents didn't approve of the parties that American children took for granted. Also they did not own a car. Just getting Madeleine to and from school events was a problem. "My parents were very strict," Madeleine Albright says today. "I could never do anything that the other kids did." Like other children who move to a new neighborhood, Madeleine wanted desperately to blend in. For years she had always been different—the exiled child in war-torn London; the daughter of the Czechoslovak ambassador in Belgrade; and now, the little refugee in America. "I always felt I was a foreigner," Albright says. That was how she thought of herself throughout her childhood.

Reading 2: Madame Ambassador

(7)   Albright understood if she were to have any chance at a higher office, she would need to spend time with people who could influence the decision. In September 1995, the United Nations was holding the fourth International Conference on Women, this time in China. Albright was appointed to lead the U.S. group. She asked **Hillary Clinton** to be the **honorary chairperson.** Each was to give a major speech at the conference. As the leader of the U.S. delegation, Albright was responsible for all the planning and scheduling, a

---

adolescence: The age that starts with the beginning of sexual development and ends with adult sexual maturity. Adolescence starts in humans around age twelve and ends about age seventeen.
Hillary Clinton: wife of U.S. President William Jefferson Clinton
honorary chairperson: The person who is selected to preside over the meetings of an organization or a committee. An "honorary chairperson" holds the title of chair but is not required to carry out any duties.

huge bureaucratic task made particularly difficult by Beijing's role as
the conference host. There was no
U.S. ambassador working in Beijing
to smooth relations with nervous
Chinese officials, who were just beginning to realize that the gathering
could become a forum for attacks
on the Communist government's
treatment of women and families.
What's more, before the conference convened, Chinese authorities

caught the Chinese **dissident** Harry Wu, who had come back to China, fo-
cusing world attention on Beijing's **poor human rights record.** There was
speculation that the U.S. group, including Mrs. Clinton, would boycott the
conference. China, which had signed up for the conference thinking it would
be like a giant fashion show, now realized that it was about to be invaded
by thousands of prominent and **assertive** women who intended to discuss
such controversial issues as human rights, more specifically the status of
women and family planning.

(8)   To the disappointment of some officials, Albright did not take a large role
in organizing U.S. participation in the conference. She did, however, make a
key political decision. Instead of arriving in China a few days before the conference to solve last minute problems, as organizers had expected, Albright
accepted an invitation to accompany the **First Lady,** who planned to arrive,
make her speech, and leave China within twenty-four hours.

(9)   Several women who attended the conference were surprised by what
they interpreted as Albright's move to **share the limelight** with Hillary Clinton. "She flew in and made a very brief appearance, the visible piece, and
then left," said one top official. "It was the first time I was consciously aware
of what a public person she was. It's also the first time I was sure she hoped
to become secretary of state. " On the other hand, few individuals turn down
a chance to travel in such exclusive company. Not only are such trips more
relaxed than ordinary commercial flights, it is an opportunity to exchange

dissident: a person who disagrees with an established religious or political system, organization, or belief
poor human rights record: The government of China has a poor record of protecting the rights of its citizens.
People who express views contrary to established government views or policies are often punished or imprisoned.
assertive: To behave assertively is to speak or act with confidence, strength, or authority.
First Lady: the title given to the wife of the president of the United States
to share the limelight: to share the spotlight; to share in the public attention

views, to get to know each other better, and talk privately without the possibility of misinterpretation by third and fourth parties.

(10)   Once in Beijing, Hillary Clinton made headlines around the world with a bold address that indirectly criticized China's harsh **family-planning policies.** It was time to "break the silence" on human rights abuses against women, she said to repeated cheers from an enthusiastic audience. "It is a violation of human rights when women are denied the right to plan their own families." When her speech was over, Mrs. Clinton flew on to Mongolia. To the annoyance of others in the U.S. delegation, Albright flew to Burma (Myanmar) to meet Daw Aung San Suu Kyi, the human rights activist and Nobel Peace Prize winner.

(11)   The next year, Albright had another opportunity to spend some airplane time with Hillary Clinton. Both women were scheduled to speak at the **American Bar Association**'s annual meeting in Orlando, Florida. The First Lady asked Albright to join her for the flight. David Scheffer, who accompanied the women, was impressed by their chemistry. "It was fascinating," he says. "They were clearly close. They joked, talked frankly, and slipped back and forth between policy issues and family talk. They each had a sense of what was important and concentrated on it, sometimes in a funny way, sometimes seriously," says Scheffer.

(12)   No one doubts that Albright's friendship with the First Lady was helpful when Albright's name came up as a possible secretary of state, but there is much more to Albright's appointment than friendship with the First Lady. Albright is a woman with whom the president and vice president were comfortable. They trusted her judgment and liked the way she expressed her opinions. Moreover, Bill Clinton always had an instinct for grand symbolic gestures, and gender issues were no exception. Clinton did not pick Albright for the job simply because she is a woman, but her sex did not hurt. He realized that the women's vote had been a big factor in his election—women had chosen him over **Republican candidate Bob Dole** by seventeen percent— and women's groups were pressuring the White House to pick a woman for one of the top cabinet jobs. "Clinton liked the idea that she was female but could be tough in the role," said Michael McCurry, Clinton's press secretary.

family-planning policies: In an effort to limit the size of its population, the Chinese government restricted family size to one child per family. Some exceptions were made to this policy: if the only child were a girl, for example, or if the family was a rural farming family, they might be allowed to have a second child. Men and women were forced to undergo sterilizations, and "extra" pregnancies were ended by abortion.
American Bar Association: an American professional organization of lawyers and judges
Republican candidate Bob Dole: Bob Dole was the Republican senator from Kansas who ran against Bill Clinton, and lost, in the 1996 American presidential election.

Comprehension Check

Check your understanding of the reading selections by marking these sentences true (*T*) or false (*F*).

___ 1. Madeleine and her family emigrated to the United States in 1948.
___ 2. The Korbel family's life in America was very similar to the life they led in Czechoslovakia.
___ 3. Madeleine started school in America in the sixth grade, although she was academically ready for the seventh grade.
___ 4. Madeleine fit in with her new schoolmates easily and became very popular.
___ 5. Madeleine Albright was the honorary chairperson of the UN's fourth International Conference on Women.
___ 6. In her speech at the conference, Hillary Clinton criticized China's human rights abuses against women.
___ 7. Hillary Clinton and Madeleine Albright have interests in common, such as politics and family matters.
___ 8. The fact that Madeleine Albright is a woman may have actually helped her become secretary of state.

Critical Thinking

Answer these questions by yourself. Then work with two or three other students to discuss the questions. Decide on a group answer to each question. Be prepared to explain your group answers to the class.

1. The Korbel family lived an "affluent" life in Czechoslovakia. What evidence does the reading give to support this statement?
2. In your opinion, what kind of life did the Korbel family live in America? Support your opinion with evidence from the reading.
3. The first reading mentions that, at age eleven, Madeleine was "an accomplished linguist." How do you think she became one? What circumstances may have helped her learn several languages so early?
4. In your opinion, what four or five things most help people to learn languages? What two things help you the most?

Word Study

 University Word List Vocabulary

academic (academically)
affluence (affluent)
bureaucracy (bureaucratic)
constant (constantly)
convene
discrete

exclude (exclusive)
fluent
frustrate
invade
linguistic (linguist)
major

prosper (prosperous)
sex
speculate (speculation)
status
symbol (symbolic)
violate (violation)

Understanding Words

Word Parts

Exercise 1: Prefixes

When the prefixes *non-*, *dis-*, and *in- / im-* are added to words, they mean *not*, *to do the opposite of*, and *the reverse of*. Add *non-*, *dis-*, or *in- / im-* to each of these words to form the words that are defined here. Write each new word on the line next to its definition. Use your dictionary if necessary.

conclusive _____   material _____

constant _____   precise _____

credit _____   secure _____

inclined _____   similar _____

_____ 1. unwilling or reluctant to do something

_____ 2. inexact; vague; general

_____ 3. not confident or sure; unsafe or unguarded; not stable

_____ 4. leading to no final result

_____ 5. unlike; different from

_____ 6. to disbelieve; to disgrace

_____ 7. unimportant; without substance or consequence

_____ 8. unstable; changeable

Ex 1-8
Ex 11+12 → Hand in

Exercise 2: Suffixes

The suffix *-able / -ible* is added to verbs to form adjectives that mean *capable of* or *tending to*. Add the correct form of the suffix *-able / -ible* to the words given (the spellings of the words may need to be altered slightly) and then use one of the new words to complete each of the following sentences. Use your dictionary if necessary.

attribute   discern   maintain   refute   verify

1. The "facts" in the case were _____. A DNA expert proved that the crime could not have been committed by the person who was accused of doing it.

2. The treaty called for a systematic and _____ reduction in the number of soldiers in the region.

3. The differences between the original painting and the reproduction were barely _____—most people would never notice them.

4. Billie Jean King's success in tennis is _____ to years of practice and training, as well as her own natural talent.

5. A very low-calorie diet will lead to quick weight loss, but the lower weight isn't generally _____ after the dieter starts eating normally again.

Exercise 3: Suffixes

The suffix *-ic* carries the meanings *having the nature of, belonging to or associated with, tending to produce*. Add the suffix *-ic* to the following words (the spellings of the words may need to be altered slightly) and then use one of the new words to complete each sentence.

academy   bureaucracy   democracy   myth   strategy

1. Obtaining a new passport and visa was a _____ nightmare. He had to fill out pages of forms, visit several offices, and pay a large fee before finally getting them.

2. His reputation in baseball was _____—no other player had ever been able to hit the ball as far as he had.

3. She decided to work toward a Ph.D. and, eventually, a professorship, because she loved the _____ life.

4. _____ placement of supports and beams made the building completely stable, even during an earthquake.

5. Equality and freedom for each individual are essential in a

_____ society.

Word Relationships

Exercise 4: Synonyms

Match each word with its synonym(s). Then write another synonym for each word on the long line provided. Use your dictionary if necessary.

__ 1. discrete   _____   a. prohibit
                                        b. greater
__ 2. exclude   _____   c. distinct
                                        d. succeed
__ 3. major   _____   e. sign
                                        f. contemplate
__ 4. prosper   _____   g. principal
                                        h. grow
__ 5. speculate _____   i. representation
                                        j. omit
__ 6. symbol   _____   k. reserved
                                        l. risk

Exercise 5: Collocations

Match items 1 through 6 with their common collocations by writing the combinations on the lines following items 1 through 6. Can you think of any other words that collocate with items 1 through 6? If so, write those combinations on the lines also.

appeal	report	scandal
accomplishment	point	symbol
attention	policy	value

1. academic

_____

_____

2. bureaucratic

_____

_____

3. constant

_____

_____

4. discrete

_____

_____

5. major

_____

_____

6. sex

_____

_____

The Grammar of Words

Exercise 6: Derivatives

Complete the chart with derivatives of the italicized words.

Noun	Noun (person)	Adjective	Adverb	Verb
academy				—
		bureaucratic		
	invader			
	—			prosper
speculation				
	—	frustrated		

Understanding Words in Sentences

Exercise 7: Word Meanings in Context

In the reading passages, scan for the words and phrases given in the following list. The number of the paragraph containing the word or phrase is given in parentheses. Circle the letter of the meaning that is most appropriate within the context of the reading passage.

1. prosperous (2)
   a. exclusive
   b. economically successful
   c. high class

2. fluent (5)
   a. speaking with wit
   b. speaking politely
   c. speaking smoothly; easily

3. discrete (5)
   a. modest
   b. separate; distinct
   c. quiet

4. convened (7)
   a. assembled; met
   b. grew strong
   c. was organized

5. exclusive (9)
   a. limited; restricted
   b. stylish; fashionable
   c. whole; undivided

6. violation (10)
   a. interruption of
   b. abuse of; harm to
   c. respect for

Exercise 8: Word Meanings in Context

Find the words in the reading passages that have the following meanings and write these words on the lines provided. Change the word form by adding or deleting a word ending if necessary. The number in parentheses is the number of the paragraph where the word occurs.

1. irritated; bothered; discouraged (3) _____

2. great in importance or interest (7) _____

3. questioning about; curiosity (7) _____

4. position or rank; condition (7) _____

5. gender, being either male or female (12) _____

6. a visible sign that represents or suggests something (12) _____

Using Words in Communication

Exercise 9: Listening

Listen to the texts on the audiotape until you understand them. Then circle the letter of the statement that best matches what you heard.

Text 1
a. Madeleine was put into fifth grade so that she could learn about "American ways."
b. Madeleine was put into sixth grade because of her age and for other reasons.
c. Madeleine was an academically excellent student and was put into seventh grade.

Text 2
a. Madeleine realized that she sounded different from other children and decided to lose her accent.
b. Madeleine was not very good at singing, and her voice always stood out.
c. Madeleine liked having a British accent because it made her different from other children at school.

Text 3

a. Madeleine Albright organized the United Nations' fourth International Conference on Women.

b. Madeleine Albright led the U.S. delegation to the UN Conference on Women.

c. Madeleine Albright went to Beijing to help plan and schedule the UN Conference on Women.

Text 4

a. Madeleine played a large role in organizing U.S. participation at the conference.

b. Madeleine arrived at the conference a few days early to solve last minute problems.

c. Madeleine made an important political decision when she decided to arrive with the First Lady, Hillary Clinton.

Text 5

a. Hillary Clinton's speech criticized the Chinese government's policies.

b. The Chinese government was very enthusiastic about Hillary Clinton's speech.

c. Women in China have the right to plan their own families.

Exercise 10: Speaking

Work with another student to ask and answer these questions.

1. As a child, did you ever move to a new place and have to change schools? How did you feel? What was positive about the experience? What was difficult about it? (If you didn't move as a child, answer the same questions about your experience of leaving home and coming to college.)

2. Madeleine Albright said that she was always "different" from other children. Why? As a child, she always felt like she was a "foreigner." Have you ever felt like this? Do you think it's important to feel like you fit in with other people? Why or why not?

3. Imagine that Madeleine is your friend. What advice would you give her about moving to a new place and going to a new school? What would you suggest that she do in order to make new friends and feel less "different" from everyone else?

Exercise 11: Reading

Madeleine Albright served as the U.S. representative to the United Nations from 1993 until she became secretary of state in 1997. How much do you know about the United Nations? Take the short quiz that follows and find out. Then look at the reading "The United Nations" and check your answers.

United Nations Quiz

1. When was the United Nations established?
   a. 1920s
   b. 1940s
   c. 1960s

2. About how many countries currently belong to the United Nations?
   a. 26
   b. 51
   c. 185

3. What does the acronym WHO stand for?
   a. World Hunger Organization
   b. World Health Organization
   c. World Humanitarian Organization

4. The largest organization in the United Nations is the
   a. General Assembly
   b. International Monetary Fund
   c. Security Council

5. The name of the organization that works for the health and welfare of children is
   a. UFO
   b. UNESCO
   c. UNICEF

The United Nations

(1)　　The United Nations began during World War II, as part of an agreement between the countries that had fought against Germany, Italy, and Japan during the war. It replaced the League of Nations as an organization for the promotion of international peace and security. Today the UN is a truly international organization. One hundred and eighty-five nations—nearly every country in the world—belong to its largest organization, the United Nations' General Assembly.

(2)　　The United Nations was formally organized, and its charter—an international treaty that sets out the basic principles of international relations—was signed on June 26, 1945, in San Francisco. This charter went into effect on October 24, 1945, with 51 original member countries. The basic UN charter contains 19 chapters that are divided into 111 articles. It provides for the organization and support of many international organizations and agencies. Today the most well-known of these organizations include the United Nations' General Assembly, the Security Council, the International Court of Justice, the World Health Organization (WHO), the International Labor Organization (ILO), the International Monetary Fund (IMF), the Educational, Scientific, and Cultural Organization (UNESCO), and the Children's Fund (UNICEF).

(3)　　According to a statement prepared by the United Nations, these "organizations work to promote respect for human rights, protect the environment, fight disease, promote development and reduce poverty. UN agencies also define the standards for safe and efficient transport by air and sea, help improve telecommunications and enhance consumer protection, work to ensure respect for intellectual property rights and coordinate allocation of radio frequencies. The United Nations leads international campaigns against illicit drug trafficking and terrorism . . . The UN and its agencies assist refugees and set up programs to clear landmines, help improve the quality of drinking water and expand food production, make loans to developing countries and help stabilize financial markets."

(4)　　In the fifty some years since its beginning, the United Nations has been successful in these and other areas. Some of its more recent achievements include

- helping to bring an end to the Iran-Iraq War
- bringing about withdrawal of Soviet troops from Afghanistan
- helping to end civil war in El Salvador

- organizing and conducting elections in Cambodia
- helping to bring an end to the system of apartheid in South Africa
- working to establish peace in Bosnia Herzegovina and Serbo-Croatia
- providing protection and assistance to refugees all over the world.

Although the activities of the United Nations are sometimes unpopular or controversial, it is difficult to imagine what the world would be like today without it.

Exercise 12: Writing

Choose one of the UN organizations or achievements given in Exercise 11 that interests you or find another topic related to the United Nations. Go to the library and consult recent encyclopedia yearbooks, the library catalogs, and periodicals or ask the reference librarian to help you locate information about this topic. You may also want to look on the Internet by using a web browser like "Infoseek." Write a three or four paragraph essay that describes this organization or event. Be sure to explain why you think your topic is important or significant.

Review Unit 2

I. Choose the correct word from the list on the left to go with each meaning. (In each set, you will not use two of the words.)

Set A

1. align
2. intervene
3. indigenous
4. impact
5. invade

___ collision; blow
___ native
___ attack

Set B

1. precede
2. role
3. speculate
4. diverse
5. execute

___ infer
___ do
___ come first

Set C

1. anthropology
2. credible
3. locate
4. deviate
5. affluent

___ well to do
___ depart from
___ believable

II. Identify the following words as synonyms (*S*) or antonyms (*A*).

___ 1. constant/irregular
___ 2. major/unimportant
___ 3. style/fashion
___ 4. positive/negative

___ 5. ultimate/primary
___ 6. eventually/ultimately
___ 7. fragment/piece
___ 8. distinct /unclear

III. Match each word on the left with a word on the right with which it often collocates.

___ 1. anthropological   a. compounds
___ 2. criminal   b. catalog
___ 3. mail-order   c. injury
___ 4. bureaucratic   d. charges
___ 5. divine   e. shift
___ 6. carbon   f. armies
___ 7. wheel   g. delays
___ 8. invading   h. intervention
     i. studies
     j. alignment

IV. Match these prefixes and suffixes with the correct words to make the words that are defined here. You may need to change the spelling of the words before adding the prefixes and suffixes. Write out each complete word in the space provided.

un-   -able   in-   dis-   -ic   -tion

_____ 1. _____ + constant = changeable; unstable

_____ 2. convene + _____ = meeting

_____ 3. _____ + locate + _____ = displacement

_____ 4. distinct + _____ = difference

_____ 5. _____ + violate = undisturbed

_____ 6. verify + _____ = defensible

V. Complete the analogies that follow with one of the words given here.

major   distinct   democracy   fuel   intuition   vertical

1. servitude : freedom :: dictatorship : _____

2. blurry : obscure :: clear : _____

3. flat : upright :: horizontal : _____

4. flag : symbol :: coal : _____

5. diverse : dissimilar :: leading : _____

6. fact : myth :: reason : _____

VI. Complete each sentence with one of the words given here.

convene   symbol   network   linguistics   role   circulate

1. Parasites often _____ in the bloodstream inside the host.

2. Once a week, the members of the commune _____ to determine policies that affect the whole group.

3. A computer _____ consists of two or more computers that are connected to one another for the purpose of communicating data electronically.

4. _____ is the scientific study of language.

5. In sociology, a _____ is the behavior expected of an individual who occupies a given social position or status.

6. In Melville's *Moby Dick,* the whale is often seen as a _____ of evil.

Unit 7
Ansel Adams

Vocabulary Preview

Preview 1

Complete each sentence with the most suitable word.

currency   evaporated   computed   found   estimate

1. Ansel helped _____ the world's first museum collection of photographs at the Museum of Modern Art in New York City.
2. Just then the sun sank below the clouds behind him, and the magic essential light _____.
3. A dealer joked, "Ansel's pictures are a new form of _____; instead of dealing in gold, we deal in *Moonrises*."
4. Very quickly, Ansel _____, in his head, the proper exposure time and shutter speed.
5. A rough _____ puts Ansel's receipts in the neighborhood of half a million dollars for the sale of fine prints of *Moonrise*.

Preview 2

Look at the way the underlined words are used in the sentences. Match each word with its definition.

1. *Speleology* is the scientific discipline that is concerned with all <u>aspects</u> of caves and cave systems.
2. Some animals, such as lizards, are able to <u>release</u> or drop off a part of the body when attacked.
3. Beautiful form, together with simplicity, characterizes the <u>traditional</u> Japanese artistic style.
4. Great effort has been <u>invested</u> in the preservation of Native American languages.
5. During meditation, logical thinking, desires, and emotional <u>attachments</u> are suspended, leaving the mind in a state of relaxed attention.

___ 1. aspects   a. to let go; to break off
___ 2. release   b. spent
___ 3. traditional   c. close ties
___ 4. invested   d. customary; having existed for a long time
___ 5. attachments   e. parts or elements of

Reading Preview: What Do You Know about Ansel Adams?

Work with two or three other students and share what you already know about these terms and phrases that are commonly used in photography.

a. camera lens   e. light filters
b. telescopic lens   f. negative
c. exposure meter   g. print
d. shutter speed   h. tripod

Work with two or three other students and share what you already know about these terms and phrases commonly associated with auctions, which are where Adams's photographs are often sold.

a. collectors   e. galleries
b. collectibles   f. auction houses
c. investors   g. sales record
d. photography dealer h. resale market

Adapted from *Ansel Adams: A Biography* by Mary Street Alinder (New York: Henry Holt, 1996), 185–90, 197–98.

Introduction to the Readings

Ansel Adams (1902–84) was an American photographer best known for his superb photographs of landscapes, particularly mountain ranges. Adams was a devoted environmentalist. His photographic books *My Camera in the National Parks, This Is the American Earth,* and *Photographs of the Southwest* are collections from the years he spent photographing the wilderness of the United States and are a fervent call for environmental preservation.

Adams is one of the outstanding technicians in the history of photography. In 1935, he published *Making a Photograph,* the first of many books he wrote on photographic techniques. One of his best-known techniques was the *zone system.* Photographers still use this method to predetermine exactly how light or dark each part of a photographed scene will be in the final print.

Adams dedicated much of his professional life to increasing public acceptance of photography as a fine art. He helped found the world's first museum collection of photographs at the Museum of Modern Art in New York City. Later, at the California School of Fine Arts in San Francisco, he established the first academic department to teach photography as a profession. The following readings are excerpts from a biography, *Ansel Adams,* by Mary Street Alinder.

Reading 1: *Moonrise, Hernandez, New Mexico:* The Photograph

(1)   For many, *Moonrise, Hernandez, New Mexico* is the greatest photograph ever made. Step into the picture. You are standing on the shoulder of Highway 84, a two-lane blacktop some thirty miles from Santa Fe. Under the last light of day, you see the village of Hernandez, nestled along the tree-lined banks of the Rio Chama, flowing down to meet the **Rio Grande. Sage** covers the ground. Burning **piñon** drifts its warm, woodsy odor from chimneys. Across the river, in the distance, stands the church of neighboring San Juan pueblo.

Rio Grande: a river that, in some stretches, divides the United States and Mexico
sage: a plant belonging to the mint family, commonly found in the American Southwest
piñon: a variety of pine tree bearing edible seeds, commonly found in the American Southwest

(2)   It is plain to see that the builders of Hernandez had reverence for God and for the earth. The adobe for the rounded walls of their church, San Jose del Chama, founded in 1835, and for their homes was extracted from the ground beneath their feet. It is Sunday. In church today, the priest and the congregation prayed for America; they could not know that **Pearl Harbor** was just a month away.

(3)   Hernandez's citizens are descendants of a few Spanish-American families with names such as Roybal and Borrego; they tend small farms that yield crops of chile and corn. A *horno,* or traditional adobe oven, sits in one backyard waiting for morning. Heaps of golden corncobs dry on the flat rooftop of one house, a ladder leaning against the wall. The corn was harvested a month ago, at night, under the light of the harvest moon; the husks are sharp and cutting by day, but their tough fabric softens in the dew of evening. Never-forgotten ancestors rest in the cemetery directly behind the backyards, the promise of life everlasting proclaimed by each white cross.

(4)   The great **vault** of the sky places Hernandez in appropriate perspective, conveying its relative insignificance. Even the snowcapped mountains only serve to punctuate the meeting of heaven and earth. You realize that the night is velvety-black and yet you can see. Each object in the scene appears to be lighted from within: village, graveyard, church, and sagebrush. Through *Moonrise,* the viewer stands beyond mankind to witness humanity's reach for the stars, for **redemption,** for God.

Reading 2: Historical and Technical Details

(5)   *Moonrise* was made on a typical Adams shooting expedition in the autumn of 1941. One Sunday, while in New Mexico to shoot a set of photographs for the Department of Interior, Ansel and his two assistants, Michael and Cedric, left their motel and drove north of Santa Fe to spend the day shooting pictures off in the Chamas River Valley. When Ansel had visited the area in 1937, he had found the landscape both challenging and photographically productive, but not so on this particular day. The sky held no promise,

---

Pearl Harbor: A surprise attack, on December 7, 1941, by the Japanese on an American military installation in Hawaii. This event brought the United States into World War II.
vault: dome; ceiling
redemption: salvation; forgiveness for sins

only the photographer's nightmare of bright, empty blue expanses (which were almost as bad as steady rain).

(6)   Throughout the whole long day Ansel wrestled, photographically speaking, with landscapes that **defied visualization.** Dusty, weary, and hungry, he and his team piled into the car and headed back to Santa Fe. They had not traveled far when Ansel glanced over his left shoulder to witness an ordinary miracle. Before him, the nearly full moon rose above Hernandez; the small cemetery with its simple white crosses reflected the last rays of the sun that was setting behind the clouds and mountains at Ansel's back. The scene provided what Ansel called "an inevitable photograph." He simultaneously steered the car into a **ditch** and slammed on the brakes, yelling all the while for Cedric and Michael to help him set up his eight-by-ten view camera. Nearly frantic, he knew that he had only seconds to act before the sun's light vanished.

(7)   Tripod set up. Camera secured. Lens attached. Film inserted. However, no exposure meter for, in all the rush, it could not be found! Perhaps only Ansel Adams could have recalled under such pressure that the **luminance** of the full moon is 250 candles per square foot, and then calculated the exposure formula; his years of hard work and technical mastery of photography had readied him for this moment. (Ansel's favorite **aphorism** paraphrased **Louis Pasteur**: "Chance favors the prepared mind.")

(8)   After computing very quickly in his head the proper exposure time and shutter speed, Ansel inserted a deep-yellow filter in front of the camera's shutter in order to darken the blue sky and lighten all yellow values, including the adobe church, the houses and the golden, autumnal hues of the changing trees. Gauging everything in place, Ansel then released the shutter. Worried that the exposure was insufficient Ansel tried for a second exposure, but just then the sun sank below the clouds behind him and the magic essential light evaporated. The creation of *Moonrise* was **serendipitous**: while a painter or sculptor can work from stored memories and imagination, something must happen in the real world for a photographer to make a photograph.

defied visualization: not lending themselves to making a good picture
ditch: a long, narrow channel on the side of the road, as for drainage
luminance: the light given off by something like a candle or the moon
aphorism: saying; proverb
Louis Pasteur: French microbiologist who originated the process used to destroy bacteria in milk (pasteurization)
serendipitous: desirable and occurring by luck or by accidental discovery

Photograph of Ansel Adams with a straight print and a fine print of *Moonrise, Hernandez, New Mexico*, 1941. Photograph © James Alinder, 1981.

Reading 3: The Price

(9)   More than either its historical or technical details, the most discussed aspect of *Moonrise* is its price. In 1980, a Boston photography dealer said, "Ansel's pictures are a new form of currency; instead of dealing in gold, we deal in *Moonrises.*" More dollars, pesos, pounds, marks, and yen have been spent on *Moonrise* than on any other image in the history of photography. A rough estimate puts Ansel's receipts in the neighborhood of half a million dollars for the sale of fine prints of *Moonrise* alone, most of the amount from 1975 onward. This is but a fraction of the profit realized by collectors and dealers in the later resale market. Once a photographer sells a fine print, he or she never sees another penny from its further sales, even if the original price is fifty dollars and ten years later it is sold for fifty thousand.

(10)   In fact, in 1948, fifty dollars was Ansel's normal price for a sixteen-by-twenty-inch *Moonrise,* including shipping. This was double the price of his other prints of similar size. Ansel's fee for a *Moonrise* was raised only slowly, to sixty dollars in 1962, seventy-five dollars in 1967, and then $150 in 1970.

(11)   As the decade of the seventies unfolded and photography grew more and more popular as a "**collectible,**" Ansel was swamped by requests for *Moonrise.* He stopped taking print orders as of December 31, 1975, his decision having been spurred by the increased demand. The negative was difficult to print, and it took him three years to fill the orders he had already taken. His last-selling price for *Moonrise* was twelve hundred dollars; after the supply was curtailed at its source, the price of a sixteen-by-twenty-inch print escalated in the secondary market of auctions and galleries to ten thousand dollars in 1980 and twenty thousand by 1996.

(12)   When significant numbers of investors began entering the photography market for the first time in the late 1970s and early 1980s, business magazines took notice. One article reported that in December 1979, the sale of a *Moonrise* for twenty-two thousand dollars at an auction house had set three sales records; it was the most ever paid for a photograph by a living photographer, the most for a twentieth-century print, and the most for a photographic work on paper. Up to that time, only a daguerreotype self-portrait by a nineteenth century photographer, on a silver-plated copper sheet, had brought more, selling for thirty-six thousand dollars. The *Wall Street Journal* even published a bar chart that allowed its investment-minded audience to compare the selling prices of *Moonrise* for the years 1977 through 1981. The current total value of all the *Moonrise* prints that Ansel made is in excess of twenty-five *million* dollars.

Comprehension Check

Check your understanding of the reading selections by marking these sentences true (*T*) or false (*F*).

___ 1. Hernandez is a village in New Mexico, near Santa Fe.
___ 2. San Jose del Chama is an old church made out of adobe bricks.
___ 3. *Moonrise,* which some regard as the greatest photograph ever made, was shot two months after the Japanese attacked Pearl Harbor.

collectible: anything that people enjoy collecting, such as dolls, coins, and paintings
Wall Street Journal: a well-known American newspaper that reports financial news

___ 4. Photographers consider bright, empty blue expanses of sky as ideal conditions for taking photographs.

___ 5. Adams could not take a second shot of *Moonrise* because the sun had sunk below the clouds and the magic essential light had evaporated.

___ 6. According to the author of the text, while painters and sculptors can work from memory, photographers can only work from images in the real world.

___ 7. The most discussed aspect of *Moonrise* is its magic quality.

___ 8. Like gold and silver, fine works of art can also serve as currency.

Critical Thinking

Answer these questions by yourself. Then work with two or three other students to discuss the questions. Decide on a group answer to each question. Be prepared to explain your group answers to the class.

1. How does a photograph become a collector's item?
2. When investors buy a work of art, what is it that they hope will happen to the purchase?
3. What would you do if you found an original print of *Moonrise*, made by Ansel Adams himself, in your grandmother's attic?

Word Study

University Word List Vocabulary

aspect	extract	negative
attach	found	perspective
compute	frantic	publish
currency	invest (investor)	release
estimate	lens	simultaneous (simultaneously)
evaporate	magic	tradition (traditional)

Understanding Words

Word Parts

Exercise 1: Prefixes and Roots

The word *perspective* comes initially from two Latin words: the prefix *per-*, meaning *through*, and the root *specere*, meaning *to look*. The following words in English have the same origin but slightly different meanings.

A. Look up these words in a dictionary and then, in your own words, write their meanings.

1. perspective

   Meaning: _____
2. perceive

   Meaning: _____
3. perceptible

   Meaning: _____

B. Use the words in part A to complete the following sentences. (Change the word form if necessary.)

1. From the judge's _____, the prosecutor had presented an excellent case.

2. The jury's _____, however, was that the prosecutor had not clearly demonstrated the guilt of the defendant.

3. The DNA evidence came from barely _____ spots of blood found on the victim's clothing.

Exercise 2: Word Families

Write the other word forms for the words given here. Work with three or four other students. Assign each other words and write sentences using those words.

Noun	Noun (person)	Adjective	Adverb	Verb
publication			—	
investment			—	
foundation				
attachment			—	
collection, collectible				
photography				

Word Relationships

Exercise 3: Associations

Underline the words in the paragraph that have to do with the field of photography. Compare your list with that written by another student.

Tripod set up. Camera secured. Lens attached. Film inserted. However, no exposure meter for, in all the rush, it could not be found! Perhaps only Ansel Adams could have recalled under such pressure that the luminance of the full moon is 250 candles per square foot, and then calculated the exposure formula; his years of hard work and technical mastery of photography had readied him for this moment. (Ansel's favorite aphorism paraphrased Louis Pasteur: "Chance favors the prepared mind.")

Exercise 4: Collocations

Write each of the following words on an index card and then write down words that often occur with that word. Trade your index cards with two or three other students to see if they can add to your list. (Remember that co-occurring words may occur before and after the given word.) In groups, write sentences using the collocations that have been written.

Example: compute: computer literate, computer terminal, and so on.
1. exposure
2. magic
3. extracted
4. traditional
5. estimated
6. released

Word Meanings

Exercise 5: The Many Meanings of *Negative*

The word *negative* has all of these meanings

a. the image that is first produced when a photograph is taken
b. an indication that some disease or condition is not present
c. an unfavorable or bad aspect
d. a statement that suggests the answer "no"
e. a negative number, one that is less than zero

Write the letter of the meaning (*a, b, c, d,* or *e*) that best fits the context of each sentence.

___ 1. He received a <u>negative</u> reply to his repeated letters and calls: the company would not consider him for the job.
___ 2. He had a <u>negative</u> attitude toward all the proposals presented by others; he would only support his own proposal.
___ 3. In sociology, rituals may be classified as positive or <u>negative.</u> A taboo is a <u>negative</u> ritual, one that is forbidden.

___ 4. An enlarger is a device used to produce photo <u>negatives</u> larger than the original negative or transparency.

___ 5. Subtracting +7 from +5 gives the <u>negative</u> answer –2.

___ 6. A skin test is considered positive when the skin becomes red and swollen and <u>negative</u> when there is no skin reaction.

Exercise 6: Derivatives

The root of the word *invest* (meaning *to install in office with great ceremony*) is *vest* from the Latin *vestis* meaning *clothing*. All of the following are words with this same root: *vest, vestments, vestry, investiture*. Use these words to complete the definitions below. Use your dictionary if necessary.

1. _____ are special clothes used by priests during church ceremonies.

2. The _____ is the room in the church where a priest keeps his special clothing.

3. A _____ is a short sleeveless garment worn over a shirt to keep warm.

4. When the president of a college is _____ he or she is formally installed in office.

5. The ceremony at which this installation takes place is called an

_____.

Exercise 7: World Currencies

Write the name of a country in which each currency is used.

1. yen   _____   6. ruble   _____

2. won   _____   7. shekel   _____

3. yuan   _____   8. bolívar   _____

4. deutsche mark _____   9. sucre   _____

5. sol   _____   10. zloty   _____

Understanding Words in Sentences

Exercise 8: Making Inferences

Very often the meaning of a word can be guessed at or *inferred* from information given in the surrounding words or sentences.

Example: It is plain to see that the builders of Hernandez had reverence for God and for the earth. The <u>adobe</u> for the rounded walls of their church was extracted from the ground beneath their feet.

From the information provided, what would you conclude is the meaning of <u>adobe</u>?
a. design
b. dirt; earth
c. wood
(The correct inference is *b. dirt; earth* because that is something that can be *extracted from the ground.*)

Infer the meaning of the underlined words from their surrounding words and sentence. Circle the letter of the correct answer.

1. Adams was a devoted <u>environmentalist.</u> His photographic books *My Camera in the National Parks, This Is the American Earth,* and *Photographs of the Southwest* are collections from the years he spent photographing the wilderness of the United States and are a fervent call for environmental preservation.

   An <u>environmentalist</u> is someone who
   a. likes to take pictures of parks and forests
   b. likes to publish books on nature
   c. likes to work on preserving our natural surroundings

2. The scene provided what Ansel called "an inevitable photograph." He <u>simultaneously</u> steered the car into a ditch and slammed on the brakes, yelling all the while for Cedric and Michael to help him set up his eight-by-ten view camera.

   To do two things <u>simultaneously</u> is to do them
   a. in sequence, one right after the other
   b. automatically
   c. at the same time

3. After computing very quickly in his head the proper exposure time and shutter speed, Ansel inserted a deep-yellow filter in front of the camera's shutter in order to darken the blue sky and lighten all yellow values, including the adobe church, the houses and the golden, autumnal hues of the changing trees. Gauging everything in place, Ansel then <u>released</u> the shutter.

When he <u>released</u> the shutter, what Ansel did was to
a. insert a color filter
b. let go of a press-down button or lever
c. adjust for shutter speed

4. Gauging everything in place, Ansel then released the shutter. Worried that the <u>exposure</u> was insufficient, Ansel tried for a second exposure, but just then the sun sank below the clouds behind him and the magic essential light evaporated.

In photography, an <u>exposure</u> is
a. a single photograph
b. a device for opening and closing the camera lens
c. a negative

5. A rough estimate puts Ansel's receipts in the neighborhood of half a million dollars for the sale of fine prints of *Moonrise* alone, most of the amount from 1975 onward. This is but a <u>fraction</u> of the profit realized by collectors and dealers in the later resale market.

A <u>fraction</u> is
a. an estimate of
b. the sum of
c. a small part of

6. His last-selling price for *Moonrise* was twelve hundred dollars; after the supply was curtailed at its source, the price of a sixteen-by-twenty-inch print <u>escalated</u> in the secondary market of auctions and galleries to ten thousand dollars in 1980 and twenty thousand by 1996.

To <u>escalate</u> is to
a. increase quickly
b. decline
c. scale

Exercise 9: Word Meanings in Context

Read the following sentences. Then complete the sentences or answer the questions by circling the letter of the correct choice.

1. The adobe for the rounded walls of their sanctuary was extracted from the ground beneath their feet.

   What was *extracted* from the ground?
   a. clay for making bricks
   b. red bricks
   c. an adobe wall

2. The great vault of the sky places Hernandez in appropriate perspective, conveying its relative insignificance.

   Which of the meanings of *perspective* best fits its use in this sentence?
   a. scale
   b. panorama
   c. attitude

3. Nearly frantic, Ansel knew he had only seconds to act before the sun's light vanished. He hurried to set up the tripod, secure the camera, attach the lens, and insert the film.

   What was driving Ansel nearly *frantic?*
   a. He might lose the right light for the picture.
   b. He might not have enough time to take several exposures.
   c. He might not have the right lens with him.

4. The negative of *Moonrise* was very difficult to print, and it took Ansel a long time to fill the orders in hand.

   Why was it hard for Ansel to fill purchase orders for *Moonrise?*
   a. It took him a long time to make a negative of the photograph.
   b. It took him a long time to make a good print from the negative.
   c. It took him a long time to deal with all the mail he was getting.

5. When significant numbers of investors began entering the photography market for the first time in the late 1970s and early 1980s, business magazines took notice.

Why would investors' interest in the photography market make business magazines take notice?
a. Business magazines would want to encourage magazine sales.
b. Business magazines would be interested in new advertising possibilities.
c. Business magazines would want to alert their readers to a new investment trend.

6. The *Wall Street Journal* even published a bar chart that allowed its investment-minded audience to compare the selling prices of *Moonrise* for the years 1977 through 1981.

The *Wall Street Journal* is
a. an investment firm
b. an accounting firm
c. a publication

Using Words in Communication

 Exercise 10: Listening

Listen to each text on the audiotape and then summarize it in two or three sentences. Try to use at least one study word in your summary.

1. _____

   _____

   _____

2. _____

   _____

   _____

3. _____

_____

_____

4. _____

_____

_____

5. _____

_____

_____

6. _____

_____

_____

Exercise 11: Reading

Read a biographical account of a well-known photographer. (Suggestions: Alfred Stieglitz, Gordon Parks, Aleksander Mikhailovich Rodchenko, Richard Avedon, Margaret Bourke-White, John Heartfield, James Van Der Zee, Pedro Meyer, Sebastião Salgado, Shoji Ueda, Kineo Kuwabara, Nobuyoshi Araki, Imogen Cunningham, Edward Weston.) Consult recent encyclopedia yearbooks, library catalogs, and periodicals or ask the reference librarian for help. You may also want to look on the Internet by using a web browser like "Google." Be prepared to give a three- to five-minute presentation about the person you choose.

Exercise 12: Speaking

Use the following questions to interview another student about the photographer he or she researched for Exercise 11.

1. Who is the photographer?
2. How did he or she get interested in or started in photography?
3. What is distinctive about his or her work?

4. What are some of his or her major accomplishments?
5. Where have his or her works been exhibited?
6. What awards has he or she won?

Give a three- to five-minute presentation to the class based on the interview.

Exercise 13: Writing

Using the questions from Exercise 12, interview another student about his or her research. Write a short essay on what you learned about the photographer during the interview. Trade essays with two or three other students. Read and comment on one another's essays.

Unit 8
Thurgood Marshall

Vocabulary Preview

Preview 1

Complete each sentence with the most suitable word.

motivated   capacity   data   liberal   diffuse

1. During his time as Supreme Court justice, Marshall continued to
   uphold his _____ views concerning the need for just treatment for American minorities.
2. The NAACP team split over whether to use social science

   _____ to make their case before the Supreme Court.
3. In his _____ as chief counsel for the NAACP, Marshall argued
   thirty-two cases before the United States Supreme Court, twenty-nine
   of which he won.
4. In the explosive arguments among lawyers with vastly different
   points of view, tempers occasionally flared, and Marshall had to

   _____ the tensions.
5. The laughs and backslapping helped, but everyone was also

   _____ by the realization that history was on the line.

Preview 2

Look at the way the underlined words are used in the sentences. Match
each word with its definition.

1. The newly constituted government promised to hold presidential
   elections every four years.
2. After listening to the evidence, all of the members of the jury concluded that the defendant was guilty.
3. Today I shall focus on the three major social reforms advocated by
   Plato in The Republic.
4. Because of the storm, people on that part of the island were deprived
   of water and electricity for over three weeks.
5. The new health care plan turned out to be vastly inferior to the one
   that the company had offered in the past.

___ 1. constitute
___ 2. conclude
___ 3. focus
___ 4. deprive
___ 5. inferior

a. to decide; to determine
b. to keep from having
c. to establish; to set up
d. lower in quality
e. to give special attention to

Reading Preview: What Do You Know about Thurgood Marshall?

Circle the correct answer. If you don't know the answer, guess.

1. Thurgood Marshall was
   a. a major league baseball player
   b. a professional basketball player
   c. an advocate for the rights of African Americans
   d. the founder of the NAACP (National Association for the Advancement of Colored People)

2. By profession, Marshall was
   a. a community action organizer
   b. a lawyer
   c. a minister
   d. a congressman

3. In 1967, Marshall was appointed
   a. Supreme Court justice
   b. president of Howard University
   c. director of the United Negro College Fund
   d. president of the NAACP

Adapted from *Thurgood Marshall: American Revolutionary* by Juan Williams (New York: Times Books, 1998), 209–27.

Introduction to the Readings

Thurgood Marshall graduated first in his class from **Howard University** in 1933 and, three years later, went to work for the National Association for the Advancement of Colored People (NAACP). In 1940 he became chief of the legal staff of the NAACP. In this capacity, he argued thirty-two cases before the United States Supreme Court, twenty-nine of which he won. Among those cases won was his "case of the century," the case of *Brown v. Board of Education of Topeka* (1954), in which **racial segregation** in American public schools was declared unconstitutional. Up until that time, African American children had been required to attend schools run separately for them.

In 1967, President Johnson nominated Marshall to the Supreme Court, an office that he held until his retirement in 1991. During his **tenure**, Marshall continued to uphold his liberal views concerning the need for just treatment for American minorities. The following excerpt is from *Thurgood Marshall: American Revolutionary*, a biography written by Juan Williams.

Reading 1: Preparing for the Case

(1)   The year leading up to the oral arguments before the Supreme Court on school segregation took a heavy toll on forty-four-year-old Thurgood Marshall. His eyes became puffy from lack of sleep and too many cigarettes. He put on weight. And he was grumpier than ever—now snapping at secretaries who were used to his good humor. Marshall got totally hooked on the school segregation case and everything else took a backseat.

(2)   No one had to tell him this was the biggest case of his career. This case could change the face of American society. Marshall began calling conferences of the brightest people from around the nation to discuss how to convince the Supreme Court that **separate but equal** was a devastating burden to black people, nothing more than racism.

Howard University: Although open to students of any race, color, or creed, Howard University in Washington, DC, was founded with the goal of providing higher education for African Americans. Today, its library is the leading research library on African American history.

racial segregation: before the Civil Rights movement, the practice of restricting African Americans to separate institutions (churches, schools) and separate facilities (parks, playgrounds, restrooms, drinking fountains, hotels, etc.)

tenure: term of office; period of time during which a position is held

separate but equal (doctrine): In theory, this doctrine, established by the Supreme Court's *Plessy v. Ferguson* ruling, held that blacks and whites could be taught separately so long as the facilities, curriculum, and so on, were the same (equal). As implemented, the doctrine focused on the "separate" and not on the "equal." Education, under this doctrine, was vastly inferior for blacks.

(3)   The NAACP team split over whether to use **social science data** to make the case before the high court. Several members of the team led the fight against anything but a serious, legal approach. Marshall disagreed. He wanted to use the social scientists' studies, particularly those of **Ken Clark.** Marshall's resolve to use studies like Clark's was rooted in his life experience—as the son of a bright man who never got an education and never became more than a waiter. Marshall saw the same trap still catching many young black people. They were defeated at a young age by limits they accepted about their talents and their right to an education.

(4)   When Marshall spoke to NAACP youth groups and asked the youngsters what they were going to do when they grew up, the kids answered: "I'm going to be a good butler" or "I hope I might be able to get in the post office." He thought to himself, that was it for them. He understood he was watching their lives get shut down before they were even grown up. He wanted to **unravel this rope** that was choking so many.

(5)   Marshall saw the crippling insecurity among those black children as a legal issue. The government, by its endorsement of segregation, was promoting self-hate in black children. He wanted to force the government to confront its own actions against American black citizens, and the schools' cases were the perfect vehicle for putting the issue in court.

(6)   As the time approached for him to argue the case, Marshall brought in more professors and lawyers to go over every possible angle and throw around ideas. "It was an amazing feat to bring in black lawyers from the South and white lawyers and historians from the law schools," said Jack Weinstein, a Columbia law professor who was helping with the case. "It almost became a national enterprise."

(7)   Conference rooms in the **Legal Defense Fund**'s offices were crammed, often with sixty or more people standing and shouting. Law books were strewn everywhere, and some people had to sit on the edges of tables because there weren't enough chairs. In this atmosphere, tempers occasionally flared, and Marshall had to diffuse the tensions. Sometimes he would

social science data: A social science is any branch of science, such as sociology or psychology, that looks at human behavior. Social science data is information gathered by social scientists in their investigations. The issue regarding the use of "social science data" was the following: many of the lawyers preparing for *Brown* wanted to focus on legal precedents, on rulings in previous cases that might help their case. Marshall did not want to stand on legalities; he wanted to use available social science data to show how harmful segregation was, from a human perspective, to African American children.
Ken Clark: social scientist whose experimental research supported Thurgood Marshall's argument that segregation is inherently unequal
to unravel this rope: to break the pattern of African American children thinking that the highest job they could aspire to was becoming a butler or a letter carrier
Legal Defense Fund: the legal arm of the NAACP

tell a joke or use his wonderful talents as a **mimic** to get everyone laughing and back to work. Despite the arguments and egos, Marshall, like the spirited conductor of an ever mobile swing band, orchestrated lively meetings. These meetings became renowned as great fun even though they involved hard work and little or no pay.

(8)   "Thurgood had an incredible gift," said June Shagaloff. "He'd have his feet up on the table, with all of these learned minds around him, in awe of him. He'd make them feel at home. He would draw out from other people their thinking, and he synthesized it and made it his."

(9)   The laughs and backslapping helped, but everyone was also motivated by the realization that history was on the line. Those gathered would work on **drafts** of the **brief** well past midnight. Every few hours someone would come out with more changes for Alice Stovall, Marshall's secretary, or one of her assistants to type into a new draft. "If I have to do this one more time"— a frustrated Stovall finally shouted to one of the other secretaries. The older woman looked at Stovall and said: "But, Alice, I don't know whether you know it, but you're helping make history here tonight. If you are asked to type that fifty times, you type it!"

Reading 2: Arguing before the Supreme Court

(10)   On December 9, 1952, a line of over two hundred people stretched beyond the cold, white marble steps leading into the Supreme Court. Many of the people had been there overnight, hoping to get a seat to hear the celebrated case. Every seat in the courtroom was filled, and the anxious crowd just about leaped to attention.

(11)   The crowd was hushed as Bob Carter rose to make the first NAACP presentation. He did not waver. He said black students in Topeka who attended segregated schools, even equally good facilities, were being denied equal educational opportunity. "The Constitution does not stop with the fact that you have equal educational facilities, but it covers the whole educational process," Carter said.

(12)   The real drama began as Marshall rose to make his oral presentation. The newspaper **the *Afro-American*** reported that "all of the Supreme Court

mimic: someone who is skilled at imitating others
drafts: successive writings of a text in order to improve it
brief: a summary of the main points to be made in a law case
Afro-American: African American newspaper founded in Baltimore in 1892

justices came to attention" when Marshall stood to speak. Even without microphones his voice boomed all around the crowded room and its high ceiling.

(13)   "We are saying that there is a denial of equal protection of the law," Marshall told the packed chamber. Inferior schools and resources were not the issue, it was segregation itself. Racial separation hurt the "development of the personalities of [black] children" and "deprived them of equal status in the school community . . . destroying their self-respect." He concluded that the "humiliation" black children went through was not "theoretical injury" but "actual injury."

(14)   Marshall pointed out that not a single lawyer from any of the states with segregated schools had refuted any of his sociological evidence of the damage done to black children. And since there was nothing to refute the point, he said, the states had an obligation to integrate their schools. All black parents wanted, Marshall said, was for state segregation laws to be ruled unconstitutional.

(15)   After the case was argued, the Supreme Court took it under consideration for a period of over two years. Marshall was beginning to suspect the court of **delaying tactics** when he received a phone call in Mobile, Alabama, in May of 1954, telling him he might want to be at the Supreme Court on May 17. Marshall caught the next train to Washington.

(16)   At 12:52 P.M. Chief Justice Earl Warren, with all the associate justices in attendance, started reading the Court's decision. As Warren began to read, Marshall was not certain which way he was going. Warren said, "In approaching this problem we cannot turn the clock back to 1868 when the **[Fourteenth] Amendment** was adopted or even to 1895 when *Plessy v. Ferguson* was written. We must consider public education in the light of its [current role] in American life."

(17)   Marshall, seated in the lawyers' section, focused a glare at Justice Stanley Reed. Marshall thought Reed, a Kentucky native, was the most likely leader of a bloc of votes to keep school segregation in place. Marshall heard that Reed had prepared a dissent, with the help of a privately hired law clerk. He wanted to watch Reed's face as a clue to what was going to happen. Reed only stared back at him, wide-eyed.

delaying tactics: legal ways, strategies, or loopholes used to postpone the vote on an issue
Fourteenth Amendment: the amendment to the U.S. Constitution that says that the right of the citizens of the United States to vote shall not be denied or abridged by the United States or by any state on account of race, color, or previous condition of servitude
Plessy v. Ferguson: It was the Supreme Court ruling on this case, in 1896, that permitted "separate but equal" public facilities.

(18)   While Marshall and Reed were **staring each other down,** Warren continued: "In these days, it is doubtful that any child may reasonably be expected to succeed in life if he is denied the opportunity of an education . . . a right which must be made available to all on equal terms . . . To separate black children from others of similar age and qualifications solely because of their race generates a feeling of inferiority as to their status in the community."

(19)   Then in dramatic style Warren made a historic pronouncement: "We conclude that in the field of public education the doctrine of 'separate but equal' has no place. Separate educational facilities are inherently unequal." Marshall recalled that when he heard those words, "I was so happy I was numb."

(20)   "When Warren read the opinion," Marshall recalled, "Reed looked me right straight in the face the whole time because he wanted to see what happened when I realized that he didn't write the dissent and I was looking right straight at him. I'm sure Reed laughed at that."

(21)   In fact, one of Reed's clerks had done research on arguments to support a possible dissent. Reed, however, decided to vote with the majority. The ruling was unanimous. "Earl Warren," said E. Barrett Prettyman, Jr., a clerk to Justice Jackson, another possible dissenter, "worked very hard, to his credit, to convince people and particularly the last one or two holdouts that it would not be in the interest of the Court or the country to have divergent views on this vital subject."

(22)   The *Afro-American*'s next edition read: SEGREGATION ILLEGAL NOW. The story quoted Marshall as saying: "It's the greatest story we ever had . . . the thing that is gratifying to me is that it was unanimous and on our side."

Courtesy of the *Michigan Daily*.

---

staring each other down: looking intently at one another in order to get the other person's attention or to convey an emotion such as anger, hate, or displeasure

Comprehension Check

Check your understanding of the reading selections by marking these sentences true (*T*) or false (*F*).

___ 1. The defense of equal voting rights for African Americans turned out to be the biggest case of Marshall's career.
___ 2. When Marshall talked to African American children he found that they had low expectations about what they could ultimately accomplish in life.
___ 3. The case that eliminated segregation in American public schools was *Brown v. Board of Education of Topeka*.
___ 4. In arguing *Brown v. Board of Education of Topeka*, Marshall used the data obtained from social scientists rather than rulings in previous court cases.
___ 5. It took the Supreme Court seven long years to arrive at its ruling on *Brown v. Board of Education of Topeka*.
___ 6. Chief Justice Reed worked hard to convince some of his colleagues that it would not be in the interest of the Court to have divergent views on the subject of school desegregation.
___ 7. In *Brown v. Board of Education of Topeka*, the Supreme Court ruled that segregated schools were inherently unequal.
___ 8. The Supreme Court vote on desegregation was unanimous.

Critical Thinking

Answer these questions by yourself. Then work with two or three other students to discuss the questions. Decide on a group answer to each question. Be prepared to explain your group answers to the class.

1. What were some of Marshall's attributes that made him an effective lawyer?
2. What were some of Marshall's less appealing attributes?
3. In your own words, explain what the issue of school desegregation was all about.

Word Study

 University Word List Vocabulary

capacity	diverge (divergent)	integrate
conclude	doctrine	liberal
constitute (constitution)	focus	mobile
data	fund	motive (motivate)
deprive	inferior	refute
diffuse	inherent (inherently)	require

Understanding Words

Word Parts

Exercise 1: Roots

The root *cap*, originating in the Latin *capere*, meaning *take*, is the stem for the following words.

capture: to take by force
captive: taken; held as a prisoner
captivity: the state of being held captive
captivate: to attract; to take someone in by virtue of one's attributes
capacity: the amount that any particular facility (such as a baseball stadium) or container (like a jar) can take or accommodate
capable: having the knowledge, skills, or ability needed to accomplish something
caption: the words printed under a picture that give information about it

Fill in each blank with one of the preceding words.

1. She was a U.S. tennis champion who combined grace and skill at the

   net to _____ eighteen Grand Slam titles.

2. The _____ under the picture of the sinking plane read: "All passengers feared lost."

3. Many considered the saintly priest _____ of performing miracles.

4. Even with a failing voice, the singer Maria Callas continued to

   _____ her fans until the time of her death.

5. Wild animals often do not reproduce in _____.

6. The carrying _____ of a habitat is the number of animals that can be supported by that particular environment.

7. The fort was _____ at dawn.

8. American prisoners of war were held _____ for several years in prison camps in Vietnam.

Exercise 2: Roots

The root *lib*, originating in the Latin *liber*, meaning *free*, is the stem for the following words.

liberty: freedom
liberal: One who is a liberal accepts many different kinds of opinions or
   actions.
liberalize: to make less strict; to allow for more freedom
liberate: to set free
liberator: one who sets others free

Fill in each blank with one of the preceding words.

1. His heroic death gave rise to the legend that he would return one day

   to _____ his people.

2. The _____ of many South American countries was Simón Bolívar.

3. The _____ Bell, a traditional symbol of U.S. freedom, was rung for the last time for George Washington's birthday in 1846.

4. Is it true that the government is going to _____ its immigration policy?

5. Conservatives with traditional, rigid ideas often find themselves in

   conflict with freethinking _____.

Exercise 3: Reviewing Prefixes

Add the prefixes *re-, dis-, de-, auto-, un-,* or *in-* to one of the following words to complete the sentences. (The spellings of the words may need to be altered slightly.) Add endings when necessary and use your dictionary if you need to. (*Note:* The *n* of the prefix *in-* often changes to the first letter of the word to which it is being added if that word begins with a consonant. [*Example: replace* changes to *irreplaceable.*])

integrate   mobile   fund   constitutional   mobilize   refutable

1. The insistence on keeping separate ethnically pure territories within

   Bosnia brought about the country's _____.

2. Was the Model T the first _____ ever manufactured by Henry Ford?

3. Many people look forward to getting a tax _____ after they file their tax return on April 15.

4. In the 1960s, laws against interracial marriages were declared

   _____ in the United States.

5. At the end of the war, the troops were quickly _____ and sent back home.

6. He claimed he had _____ evidence for the harmful effects of school segregation on the self-image of African American children.

Exercise 4: Suffixes

A.

What nouns are formed by adding *-(t)ion* to the following words? (The spellings of the words may need to be altered slightly.) Use your dictionary if necessary.

1. deprive   _____

2. diffuse   _____

3. integrate   _____

4. conclude   _____

5. constitute   _____

B.

Now, use either the noun *or* verb form of one of the preceding words to complete the following sentences. Add word endings when necessary.

1. For many years, Native Americans were _____ of the right to vote.

2. The data we have at present do not support your _____.

3. One of the major goals of the Civil Rights movement was the fuller

   _____ of African Americans into American society.

4. He intends to _____ his speech with these famous words of Socrates: *The unexamined life is not worth living.*

5. Ultimately, most nineteenth-century immigrants were able to

   _____ easily into American culture.

6. In the _____ light of the room, we could hardly see anything.

7. He was always boasting about his healthy _____. "I've never been sick a day in my life," he would say.

8. Illegal wire-tapping _____ a violation of our civil rights.

9. During the displacement brought about by the war, many of the

   refugees suffered extreme _____.

10. The Internet has accelerated the _____ of ideas and information beyond our greatest expectations.

Word Relationships

Exercise 5: Synonyms

Cross out the word in each series that is not a synonym for the first word in that series. Use your dictionary if necessary.

1. inherent	inborn	innate	built in	extrinsic
2. inferior	preferred	lesser	lower	subordinate
3. doctrine	heresy	dogma	faith	principle
4. diverge	split	unite	bend	divide
5. deprive	endow	remove	deny	disinherit
6. mobile	portable	moving	stationary	ambulatory

Exercise 6: Synonyms and Antonyms

Identify the following pairs of words as synonyms (*S*) or antonyms (*A*).

___ 1. capacity/aptitude   ___ 5. fund/finance

___ 2. conclude/terminate   ___ 6. motivate/discourage

___ 3. refute/corroborate   ___ 7. focus/center

___ 4. diffuse/disperse   ___ 8. inherent/external

Exercise 7: Collocations

Here are some common collocations. With a partner, identify the context in which you are likely to hear or read the collocation. Then, write a definition for each collocation.

1. liberal arts   Context:_____

     Meaning: _____

2. educationally deprived   Context: _____

     Meaning: _____

3. entrance requirements   Context: _____

     Meaning: _____

4. data processing   Context: _____

     Meaning: _____

5. slush fund   Context: _____

     Meaning: _____

6. liberal education   Context: _____

     Meaning: _____

7. required courses   Context: _____

     Meaning: _____

8. database   Context: _____

     Meaning: _____

Word Meanings

Exercise 8: Using Words Correctly

Many words have more than one meaning. Consider these three meanings of *conclude.*

a. to say the last thing you want to say; to bring to an end

   Example: He concluded the meeting with a plea for money to help the refugees.

b. to decide that something is true on the basis of all the information at hand

   Example: From his mathematical computations, Kepler concluded that the movement of the planets around the sun was not circular but elliptical.

c. to come to a formal agreement; to settle something finally

   Example: The treaty that was concluded between Mexico and the United States gave the U.S. approximately 500,000 square miles of the North American continent.

Look at the way the word *conclude* or its derivative is used in the following sentences and then write the letter of the meaning that best fits each sentence.

___ 1. What was his *conclusion,* that she was innocent or that she was guilty?
___ 2. In *conclusion,* he said a prayer for the victims of the earthquake.
___ 3. The Constitution does not specifically give a president power to *conclude* executive agreements.
___ 4. His actions set in motion the happy events that *concluded* the play.
___ 5. Some authorities have *concluded* that marijuana is harmful.
___ 6. A commercial agent is one who negotiates and *concludes* contracts on behalf of his or her employer.

___ 7. In Judaism, the prescribed period of mourning begins immediately after the burial and *concludes* with sundown on the seventh day.

___ 8. The judge *concluded* that the accused was insane and, therefore, not responsible for his actions.

___ 9. From the data, social scientists *concluded* that African American children have a low estimation of their self-worth.

Understanding Words in Sentences

Exercise 9: Word Meanings in Context

Reread the following passages from the introduction to the readings and the reading selections. Then complete the sentences or answer the questions by circling the letter of the correct choice.

1. Among those cases won was his "case of the century," the case of *Brown v. Board of Education of Topeka* (1954), in which racial segregation in American public schools was declared unconstitutional. Up to that time, African American children had been required to attend schools run separately for them.

   Prior to the *Brown* case, African American children were required to
   a. attend racially segregated schools
   b. attend integrated schools
   c. pay tuition for their schooling

2. Thurgood Marshall graduated first in his class from Howard University in 1933 and, three years later, went to work for the National Association for the Advancement of Colored People (NAACP). In 1940 he became chief of the legal staff of the NAACP. In this capacity, he argued thirty-two cases before the United States Supreme Court.

   In what capacity did Marshall serve the NAACP?
   a. as president of the NAACP
   b. as clerk to the legal staff of the NAACP
   c. as the lawyer in charge of all the legal work carried out by the NAACP

3. The year leading up to the oral arguments before the Supreme Court on school segregation took a heavy toll on forty-four-year-old Thurgood Marshall. His eyes became puffy from lack of sleep and too many cigarettes. He put on weight. And he was grumpier than ever—now snapping at secretaries who were used to his good humor.

In this context, the idiom *took a heavy toll* means
a. had a damaging, negative effect on Marshall
b. demanded a lot of mental work from Marshall
c. made Marshall gain a lot of weight

4. As the time approached for him to argue the case, Marshall brought in more professors and lawyers to go over every possible angle and throw around ideas.

Marshall brought together many professors and lawyers
a. to consider different perspectives, or points of view, on the subject of segregation
b. to share and discuss ideas on the topic
c. both of the above

5. The Court's ruling on segregation was unanimous. Justice Warren had worked very hard, to his credit, to convince people and particularly the last one or two holdouts that it would not be in the interest of the Court or the country to have divergent views on this vital subject.

What Justice Warren had been able to do was to
a. get everyone to work very hard
b. get everyone to vote the same way
c. get the American people to agree with the court's ruling

Exercise 10: Idioms

Idioms are formulaic expressions that are used as a whole and have a very specific culture-bound meaning. Here are some examples that appear in the reading selections. Without using a dictionary, work with two other students at guessing their meanings from the context. Write the meanings on the lines provided.

a. took a backseat (1)

Meaning: _____

b. feel at home (8)

Meaning: _____

c. caught the train (15)

Meaning: _____

d. turn the clock back (16)

Meaning: _____

Using Words in Communication

Exercise 11: Listening

Listen to the following texts about Thurgood Marshall. Fill in the missing words in each sentence. Check your answers against those of another student.

1. William Marshall, his father, told Thurgood from an early age to treat

    everyone with _____ but never to let any _____ go by without standing up for himself.

2. As part of the protective blanket she wrapped around _____,

    Grandma Mary also gave him practical _____ about his

    _____ as a young black man in turn-of-the century

    _____. "Your mother and father want you to be a dentist or a

    doctor, something like that," she told him. "And I _____ you make it. But just in case you don't, I'm going to teach you how to

    _____. And you know why? You've never seen an

    _____ black cook."

3. Colored High and Training School was Baltimore's first high school for

   _____. The school had no _____, no _____,

   and no _____ when Thurgood arrived. "The school's in

   urgent need of _____. It is sadly short of anything like an

   adequate _____," the principal had written in his

   _____ report to the superintendent of public instruction.

4. At age sixteen, Thurgood _____ began to change. The teasing,

   often goofy boy began a _____ of experiences that opened his

   eyes to the painful _____ of economic and _____
   problems crippling most black Americans.

5. Marshall returned from his trips to the Deep _____ more

   _____ than ever of the need to _____ the

   _____ laws that kept southern blacks poor and _____.

Exercise 12: Speaking

With another student, take turns asking and answering the following
questions. When you finish, change partners and go through the questions and answers again with your new partner.

a. What does the term *civil rights* mean to you?
b. Is there a formal document in your country that protects people's
   rights? What is it called?
c. Which rights are protected?
d. What actions are considered unconstitutional?
e. What is your government required to do if your rights are violated?

Exercise 13: Reading

Read the following amendments to the Constitution of the United States
and the dates on which the amendments were passed. Then answer the
questions.

Amendments Thirteen to Twenty-One of the U.S. Constitution

The Thirteenth Amendment (1865)
Neither slavery nor involuntary servitude shall exist within the United States, or any place subject to their jurisdiction.

The Fifteenth Amendment (1870)
The right of citizens of the United States to vote shall not be denied or abridged by the United States or by any state on account of race, color, or previous condition of servitude.

The Seventeenth Amendment (1913)
The Senate of the United States shall be composed of two Senators from each state, elected by the people thereof, for six years, and each Senator shall have one vote.

The Eighteenth Amendment (1919)
After one year from the ratification of this article, the manufacture, sale, or transportation of intoxicating liquors is hereby prohibited.

The Nineteenth Amendment (1920)
The rights of citizens of the United States to vote shall not be denied or abridged by the United States or by any state on account of sex.

The Twenty-first Amendment (1933)
The eighteenth article of Amendment to the Constitution of the United States is hereby repealed.

Which amendment protects an American citizen from each of the actions described here? Write the number of the appropriate amendment in the blank to the left.

___ 1. in 1890, being used as a slave for planting cotton
___ 2. in 1924, making it difficult for women to vote in a local election
___ 3. in 1934, jailing a person for importing beer from one state to another
___ 4. in 1932, allowing a new state only one senator when joining the Union
___ 5. in 1967, making it difficult for Hispanics to vote in a county election
___ 6. in 1921, trying to force someone to serve liquor at a wedding reception

Exercise 14: Writing

Brown v. Board of Education of Topeka brought about great social changes in America. Was there a court case or an event in your country that brought about great social change? Write a short essay that describes how and why the change happened.

Unit 9
Frank Lloyd Wright

Vocabulary Preview

Preview 1

Complete each sentence with the most suitable word.

adjacent   reinforce   oscillate   subside   interlocking

1. Wright thought that a building foundation made of short

   _____ pieces of concrete would be more flexible during an
   earthquake.

2. During an earthquake, deep foundations tend to _____ with
   the wave motion of the earth, causing buildings to rock back and forth.

3. The enormous weight of the concrete foundation caused the Tokyo

   Imperial Hotel to _____ into the soft, muddy soil.

4. The drawings Wright showed Kaufmann helped to _____ the
   unusual and beautiful design he had planned for "Fallingwater."

5. Mr. Kaufmann originally wanted "Fallingwater" built _____
   to Bear Run Creek, rather than over it.

Preview 2

Look at the way the underlined words are used in the sentences. Match
each word with its definition.

1. Police officers wear special protective vests, called "body armor," to
   help <u>deflect</u> bullets during a gunfight.
2. The girl's reflection was badly <u>distorted</u> because the mirror was old
   and dirty.
3. The doctor suggested that he <u>modify</u> his diet by eliminating fats,
   sugars, and salt in order to lose weight.
4. Government spending failed to <u>revive</u> the economy, and the recession
   continued.
5. Modern homes are full of appliances that <u>utilize</u> electricity.

___ 1. deflect

___ 2. distorted

___ 3. modify

___ 4. revive

___ 5. utilize

a. to change slightly; to adjust

b. to turn aside; to turn off course

c. to make use of; to use

d. misshapen or twisted

e. to restore; to bring back to life

Reading Preview: What Do You Know about Frank Lloyd Wright?

Circle the answer. If you don't know the answer, guess.

1. Frank Lloyd Wright is famous for
    a. helping his brothers, Orville and Wilbur, invent the airplane
    b. architectural designs that integrate buildings with their surroundings
    c. inventing new materials, like concrete, for building construction

2. Frank Lloyd Wright was
    a. born in the 1860s in Richland Center, Wisconsin
    b. the youngest of three children
    c. raised by his father, after his parents divorced

3. Frank Lloyd Wright designed
    a. the Empire State and Chrysler Buildings
    b. the Johnson Wax Building and the "Fallingwater" house
    c. the Golden Gate Bridge and the Sears Tower

Adapted from *Many Masks: A Life of Frank Lloyd Wright* by Brendan Gill (New York: Putnam, 1987), 257–64 and 344–54.

Introduction to the Readings

Frank Lloyd Wright, born in 1867 in Richland Center, Wisconsin, created a truly unique, modern, American style of architecture. His buildings are known for their dramatic, clean lines and often unusual settings. Although Wright designed many innovative commercial buildings, his "Prairie Homes," built in several midwestern American cities, are equally famous. The readings here, adapted from Brendan Gill's Many Masks: A Life of Frank Lloyd Wright, are about two of Wright's most famous buildings: the Tokyo Imperial Hotel in Japan and the unique "Fallingwater" house in Bear Run, Pennsylvania.

Reading 1: The Imperial Hotel

(1)   The Imperial Hotel, built in Tokyo in 1922 and eventually torn down in 1967, was one of Wright's most significant works. The chief fame of the Imperial Hotel comes from its having survived the **great earthquake of 1923,** but the hotel was also known for its vast public spaces and unusual interior decoration. The **Mayan themes,** which had manifested themselves in some of Wright's earlier buildings, were also present here—done beautifully in local stone.

(2)   From the beginning, Wright was aware that earthquakes were common in Japan. In his designs for the hotel he would have to confront what he described as "this terrible natural enemy of all building—**the tremblor!**" In his autobiography he wrote: "For more than four years, I worked upon it . . . I studied the tremblor. Found it a wave-movement, not of sea, but of earth. Because of the wave movements, deep foundations like long **piles** would **oscillate** and rock the structure. Therefore the foundation should be short or shallow. There were sixty or seventy feet of soft mud below the eight feet of surface soil. The mud seemed a good cushion to relieve the terrible shocks.

great earthquake of 1923: The Japanese cities of Tokyo and Yokohama were severely damaged by a huge earthquake in 1923.
Mayan themes: The Maya are an Indian people from Central America. Frank Lloyd Wright used images and designs from their art in his work.
the tremblor: Frank Lloyd Wright's term for an earthquake, because the earth seems to tremble or shake during an earthquake
piles: A long slender column of wood, steel, or concrete that is driven into the ground. Piles support the vertical weight or load of a building.
oscillate: to rock or sway back and forth

Photograph of the Imperial Hotel courtesy The Frank Lloyd Wright Archives, Scottsdale, AZ.

Why not float the building upon it? Why not a building made like two hands thrust together palms inward, fingers interlocking and yielding to movement—but resilient enough to return to its original position when the distortion ceased?"

(3)   With the assistance of Paul Mueller, Wright set about floating his vast structure on a couple of thousand short, close-set concrete fingers. Wright's **protégé,** Antonin Raymond, claimed that the fingers never really worked and that what Mueller and Wright wound up with was an immense concrete slab resting on mud. Regardless of the truth, the project continued year after year, with Wright constantly changing his plans according to the capacities of the indigenous Japanese workforce and his ever-increasing knowledge of what the hotel would need to have in order to serve both its foreign and Japanese clients.

(4)   Though the hotel was not yet finished, Wright left Tokyo for the last time in 1921. The famous **sequel** to the building of the Imperial Hotel came two

protégé: a person who is trained and guided in his or her career by an experienced or influential person
sequel: something that comes after an event or a situation; the continuation of a book or film

years later, when Tokyo and Yokohama suffered devastation in the greatest earthquake in Japanese history. According to Raymond, the hotel did suffer some comparatively minor damage; what is more important to history is that an overwhelming majority of the steel-framed buildings in Tokyo easily survived the earthquake and that Wright's "floating" foundation was no more successful in resisting the earthquake than the conventional foundations of other steel-framed buildings. Moreover, over the years, the great weight of the hotel caused it to subside, or sink, continuously on its unstable concrete foundation, in some places to a depth of four feet. The high cost of maintaining the basic utilities of the hotel **in the face of** this subsidence was one of the chief reasons for its demolition in 1967. The hotel was gorgeous, but it was by no means the engineering marvel that Wright said it was.

Reading 2: Fallingwater

(5)   In 1934, an exceptionally intelligent young man of twenty-four named Edgar J. Kaufmann, Jr., was attracted to Wright's **Taliesin Fellowship** in Wisconsin. Kaufmann's parents owned a beautiful piece of wilderness property on a stream called Bear Run, in the mountains some sixty miles south of Pittsburgh, Pennsylvania. They were accustomed in summer to **"roughing it"** at a camp near the stream, and they asked Wright to design an all-year-round country house for them there. Wright visited the site and noted, among other things, a very large and smooth **boulder** overhanging the waterfall which was Bear Run's most remarkable feature. A map of the site was sent to Wright during the winter of 1935, along with word that the Bear Run house should be planned to cost between twenty and thirty thousand dollars. To Kaufmann's distress, many weeks passed and no drawings or plans emerged from the studio workshop at Taliesin. Mr. Kaufmann, Sr., had scheduled a business trip to the Midwest, and he telephoned Wright, saying that he would like to drop in at Taliesin and see Wright's drawings and plans for the house at Bear Run.

in the face of: as a result of; because of
Taliesin Fellowship: Located in Spring Green, Wisconsin, and established by Wright in 1932, Taliesin was an artistic community and school where "fellows" (students) worked and studied with Wright. Wright also had his family home here.
roughing it: living or doing something under harsh, primitive conditions
boulder: a huge rock

(6)   We may choose to believe any of several accounts of what happened next; all are equally admiring of Wright's coolness in a moment of crisis. According to **Tafel's** recollection, Wright said, "Come along! We're ready for you." Overhearing the words, Wright's assistants were shocked, for they felt sure that Wright had not yet drawn a single line on the Bear Run project. The next morning Kaufmann called again; he was in Milwaukee and would be driving at once to Taliesin. The trip should take him no more than two hours and ten minutes. Tafel describes the scene:

(7)   "Wright hung up the phone, sat down at the table set with the **plot plan** and started to draw. First floor plan. Second floor. **Section, elevation.** The design just poured out of him . . . Pencils were used up as fast as we could sharpen them . . . Erasures, overdrawing, modifying. Then, the bold title across the bottom: 'Fallingwater.' The name simply, and delightfully, reversed the word *waterfall.*

(8)   Just before noon Mr. Kaufmann arrived. He was greeted graciously by the master, 'We've been waiting for you.' The description of the house, its setting, its philosophy, poured out. Poetry in form, line, color, textures, and mediums: a reality to live in. They went up to the hill garden dining room for lunch, and while they were away **Bob Mosher** and I drew up the other two elevations, naturally in Mr. Wright's style. When they came back, Mr. Wright continued describing the house, using the new elevations to reinforce his presentation. Second thoughts? The basic design never changed—pure all the way."

(9)   Fallingwater is an astonishing house. It stands, or appears to stand, upon air. Projecting out over Bear Run by means of almost invisible concrete supports, the house and its terraces seem to float above the waterfall. Wright said of the house, "I think you can hear the waterfall when you look at the design. At least it is there, and Kaufmann will live in intimacy with the thing he loves." The only mild objection that Kaufmann raised to the unusual structure was that he had supposed it would be located on the opposite side, adjacent to Bear Run, where it would offer a pleasing view of the waterfall. Wright made no effort to disguise the fact that the house, as he had designed it, was in the one place where it would be impossible to view the

Tafel: Edgar Tafel was an apprentice at Taliesin.
plot plan: a drawing that shows the physical features of a piece of land
section: a drawing that shows a building as if it were cut open, so one can see the interior
elevation: a drawing that shows the building in three dimensions
Bob Mosher: Bob Mosher was an apprentice at Taliesin.

waterfall. On the contrary, he emphasized the peculiarity, saying, "I want you to live with the waterfall, not just look at it."

(10)   Edgar Kaufmann has written, "It was an extraordinary moment when the full force of Wright's concept became apparent . . . We did not hesitate; whatever the previous expectations and whatever the problems suggested by the plans . . . The prospects were exhilarating."

Reading 3: Building Fallingwater

Photograph of Fallingwater by Robert P. Ruschak courtesy of the Western Pennsylvania Conservancy.

(11)   It was only when the actual building of the house began that exhilaration gave way to alarm and sometimes to anguish. At one point, on the advice of Pittsburgh engineers, and without Wright's permission, more steel reinforcing

rods were introduced into the **main-floor slab** than Wright's plans called for. On discovering this Wright wrote a furious letter to Kaufmann:

> I am not willing to be insulted . . . I have put so much more into this house than you or any other client had a right to expect that if I haven't your confidence—to hell with the whole thing . . .

The sentence beginning "I have put so much more into this house . . ." is almost word for word the same angry cry that Wright had uttered to his previous clients Darwin D. Martin and Aline Barnsdall. In each case the clients also felt the same way and uttered approximately the same angry cry. Architect and client would become locked in a struggle that neither was willing to end.

(12)   Kaufmann learned quickly how to deal with Wright; his reply to Wright's outburst was brilliant. He wrote:

> Now don't you think we should stop writing letters and that you should come to Pittsburgh and clear up the situation by getting the facts? It is difficult for me to conceive that a man of your magnitude and understanding could write such a letter. Out of respect for our past association I must naturally put your letter aside as if it had never been written.

(13)   So, the building continued to rise. Out of Wright's and Kaufmann's disagreements and compromises emerged one of the most interesting houses on earth. Its appearance aside, Fallingwater is also of interest because it helped revive Wright's reputation as America's greatest living architect. It reveals the degree to which Wright had been keeping up with his contemporaries in the profession.

(14)   The risks assumed in the **siting** and construction of Fallingwater were more than justified by its appearance and by the pleasure the Kaufmanns and their guests took in the house. Nevertheless, the risks were real, and Kaufmann himself never felt sure that the building was safe. Cracks would appear in the concrete and be mended and reappear; deflections of the **cantilevered terraces** could be seen by the naked eye, though most of

main-floor slab: the foundation, or floor of the main level of the house
siting: location, choice of building site
cantilevered terraces: a terrace is a porch or raised level area that adjoins a house. If a terrace is "cantilevered," it projects out into space and is supported underneath by beams and brackets called "cantilevers."

them were minor and were caused by changes in temperature from season to season. Edgar J. Kaufmann, Jr., was impatient with the idea that the structure's flaws amount to a serious criticism of Wright's planning. He writes, "The architect and his client knew the design of Fallingwater was an exploration beyond the limits of **conventional** practice . . . Some of the great monuments of architecture have suffered structural troubles, precisely because they were striving beyond normal limitations . . . Yet these buildings still stand and add glory to their countries and their art. My father was no monarch and his house is not a public monument, but Wright's genius justifies these references. No apologies are necessary for what he achieved at Fallingwater."

Comprehension Check

Check your understanding of the reading selections by marking these sentences true (*T*) or false (*F*).

___ 1. Wright used Mayan themes for the first time in his design for the Tokyo Imperial Hotel .

___ 2. Wright designed a special foundation to help the hotel survive earthquakes.

___ 3. The Imperial Hotel was one of the only steel-framed buildings in Tokyo that survived the earthquake of 1923.

___ 4. A huge boulder made it impossible for Wright to build a house at the Bear Run site.

___ 5. Mr. Kaufmann named the house "Fallingwater."

___ 6. Wright had serious disagreements with many of his clients but not with Mr. Kaufmann.

___ 7. "Fallingwater" showed that Wright was truly one of America's greatest architects.

___ 8. Mr. Kaufmann loved the design of the house, but he was never completely sure that the structure was safe.

conventional: accepted; usual; ordinary

Critical Thinking

Answer these questions by yourself. Then work with two or three other students to discuss the questions. Decide on a group answer to each question. Be prepared to explain your group answers to the class.

1. In your own words, explain Wright's design for the foundation of the Tokyo Imperial Hotel and the reasons he designed it that way. Was this design successful? Why or why not?
2. What kind of personality or character do you think Wright had? Support your opinion with evidence from the readings.
3. "Fallingwater" is one of the most well known of Frank Lloyd Wright's buildings. What made this building so significant?

Word Study

 University Word List Vocabulary

adjacent	interlock	oscillate
construct (construction)	intimacy	reinforce
contrary	magnitude	revive
deflect (deflection)	manifest	subside
distort (distortion)	modify	texture
imperial	monarch	utilize (utilities)

Understanding Words

Word Parts

Exercise 1: Prefixes

The prefixes *sub-* and *super-* have basically opposite meanings. *Sub-* means *under, beneath,* or *below,* while *super-* means *over, above,* or *in addition.* Complete the following sentences by writing either *sub* or *super* in the blank within each sentence. Then write the entire newly formed word on the line provided. Use your dictionary if necessary.

1. The "hippie" movement of the 1960s was a _____ culture that became associated with rock music, drugs, colorful fashions, and the antiwar protests of some young Americans.

   New word: _____

2. Sigmund Freud divided the human psyche into three parts: the id, the ego, and the _____ ego.

   New word: _____

3. The land was _____ divided into four lots, each with an area of about one acre.

   New word: _____

4. The heading "Events in the News" was followed by the _____ headings "International," "National," and "Local."

   New word: _____

5. Some analysts predict that China will become the next _____ power in world politics.

   New word: _____

6. The term *marine* refers to the ocean or sea; therefore a ship that travels

   in the sea, under the water, is called a _____ marine.

   New word: _____

7. The photograph was unusual; one image of the mountain had been

   _____ imposed on top of another.

   New word: _____

8. Wright's apprentices at Taliesin were _____ ordinate to him; that is, they worked under his guidance and followed his directions.

   New word: _____

Exercise 2: Suffixes

The suffix -*ary* comes to English from the Latin -*arius* and the French -*aire,* meaning *related to* or *connected with.* It is added to nouns to form adjectives. Combine each of the following words with -*ary* to form a new word (altering their spellings slightly if necessary). Write the meaning of the new word on the line provided. Use your dictionary if necessary.

1. fragment   +   ary   = _____

   Meaning: _____

2. militia   +   ary   = _____

   Meaning: _____

3. rudiment   +   ary   = _____

   Meaning: _____

4. station   +   ary   = _____

   Meaning: _____

5. sum   +   ary   = _____

   Meaning: _____

6. volunteer   +   ary   = _____

   Meaning: _____

Word Relationships

Exercise 3: Synonyms

Match each word on the left with its synonym. Then write another synonym for each word on the long line provided. Use your dictionary if necessary.

__ 1. contrary   _____   a. royal

__ 2. construct   _____   b. size

__ 3. imperial   _____   c. sovereign

__ 4. intimacy   _____   d. employ

__ 5. magnitude   _____   e. opposite

__ 6. monarch   _____   f. closeness

__ 7. texture   _____   g. build

__ 8. utilize   _____   h. feel

Exercise 4: Analogies

Use one of the words from the word lists in Units 7, 8, or 9 to complete the analogy. Change the word form by adding a word ending if necessary.

1. still : stationary :: movable : _____

2. want : desire :: need : _____

3. right : conservative :: left : _____

4. preserve : maintain :: change : _____

5. over : under :: superior : _____

6. food : flavor :: fabric : _____

Exercise 5: Collocations

In each set of words, match the word on the left with the word or phrase on the right with which it often collocates. (In each set, you will not use one of the words.)

Set A

__ 1. adjacent   a. image
__ 2. approximate   b. room
__ 3. reinforced   c. monarchy
__ 4. distorted   d. concrete
                          e. amount

Set B

__ 5. oscillate   f. to expectations
__ 6. modify   g. against all odds
__ 7. contrary   h. between two points
__ 8. magnitude   i. a design
                          j. of the situation

Set C

__ 9. deflected   k. parts
__ 10. interlocking   l. proclamation
__ 11. intimate   m. light
__ 12. imperial   n. destiny
                          o. relationship

Word Meanings and Forms

Exercise 6: Word Forms

Complete each sentence with the correct word.

1. Dr. Hewett and his team found shards, or _____, of a type of pottery that had not been found in the Southwest before.
   fragment   fragmented   fragments   fragmentary

2. The secretary of state attempts to resolve political disputes without the use of _____ force.
   militia   militant   military   militarize

3. It is difficult to speak a language without learning the _____ of its grammar.
   rudiment   rudiments   rudimentary   rudimentarily

4. Buildings are generally _____ objects, but the motion of the earth makes them move quite a bit during an earthquake.
   station   stationary   stationers   stationery

5. Be sure to _____ the main ideas in the final paragraph of your essay.
   sum   summary   summation   summarize

6. Working on the farm at Taliesin was not _____; students were expected to do about four hours of work a day as part of their "tuition."
   volunteers   voluntary   voluntarism   voluntaries

Understanding Words in Sentences

Exercise 7: Word Meanings in Context

Find the words in the text that have the following meanings and write these words on the lines provided. Change the word form by adding or deleting a word ending if necessary. The number in parentheses is the number of the paragraph where the word occurs.

1. important; significant notable (1) _____

2. to oppose; to face a challenge (2) _____

3. sinking or settling downward (4) _____

4. critical event; turning point (6) _____

5. to turn opposite; to turn back to front (7) _____

6. personal manner; distinctive method (8) _____

7. customer (11) _____

8. stature; size; greatness (12) _____

Exercise 8: Word Meanings in Context

Reread the following passages from the text. Then complete the sentences or answer the questions by circling the letter of the correct choice.

1. Kaufmann's parents owned a beautiful piece of wilderness property on a stream called Bear Run, in the mountains some sixty miles south of Pittsburgh, Pennsylvania . . . Wright visited the site and noted, among other things, a very large and smooth boulder overhanging the waterfall which was Bear Run's most remarkable feature.

   The most unusual thing about the Bear Run site was
   a. the mountains
   b. the large, smooth rock
   c. the waterfall

2. To Kaufmann's distress, many weeks passed and no drawings or plans emerged from the studio workshop at Taliesin. Mr. Kaufmann, Sr., had scheduled a business trip to the Midwest, and he telephoned Wright, saying that he would like to drop in at Taliesin and see Wright's drawings and plans for the house at Bear Run.

   Mr. Kaufmann was concerned because
   a. he had scheduled a business trip to the Midwest
   b. several months had passed and he had seen no drawings
   c. he wanted to visit Wright at Taliesin

3. We may choose to believe any of several accounts of what happened next; all are equally admiring of Wright's coolness in a moment of crisis. According to Tafel's recollection, Wright said, "Come along! We're ready for you." Overhearing the words, Wright's assistants were shocked, for they felt sure that Wright had not yet drawn a single line on the Bear Run project.

   Why were Wright's assistants shocked?
   a. Wright told Tafel the designs were not ready
   b. they overheard him talking with Tafel
   c. they were sure that Wright had not done any drawings for Bear Run

4. Wright hung up the phone, sat down at the table set with the plot plan and started to draw. First floor plan. Second floor. Section, elevation. The design just poured out of him . . . Pencils were used up as fast as we could sharpen them . . . Erasures, overdrawing, modifying. Then, the bold title across the bottom: "Fallingwater." The name simply, and delightfully, reversed the word *waterfall.*

   The name of the Bear Run project
   a. was chosen by Kaufmann
   b. came from the main feature of the site—the waterfall
   c. was not chosen until after the house was built

5. The best title for these paragraphs is
   a. The Fallingwater Project
   b. Building in the Wilderness
   c. Naming a House

Using Words in Communication

 Exercise 9: Listening

First, just listen to the text. Then, listen a second time and take notes. Do not try to write every word; just write down important ideas, words, or phrases. Then, working on your own or with another student, try to rewrite the original text from your notes. When you have finished, compare what you wrote with what other students have written. Finally, listen to the text one more time to check what you have written.

1. _____

   _____

   _____

2. _____

   _____

   _____

3. _____

   _____

   _____

4. _____

   _____

   _____

Exercise 10: Reading

Read the texts and then complete the exercises that appear after each text. When you are finished, discuss your answers with another student.

The Beth Shalom Synagogue—Part 1

(1)   One of the most important events in Wright's career was the designing of the Beth Shalom **Synagogue,** in Elkins Park, an affluent suburb of Philadelphia. Of all Wright's buildings Beth Shalom was the closest to being a collaboration between the individual who commissioned it and the architect who designed it. This alliance is surprising: Mortimer J. Cohen, the **rabbi** who commissioned the temple, had a national reputation as a scholar, speaker, and author, but he didn't paint or draw and his knowledge of the architecture of synagogues was based upon his study of Jewish history. And yet Wright consented to call Cohen the co-designer of Beth Shalom and to put Cohen's name beside his own.

synagogue: A building where Jewish people meet to worship or study their religion. A synagogue is also called a "temple."
rabbi: A Jewish religious leader. A rabbi may lead a synagogue, or be qualified to teach Judaism or Jewish law.

(2)   In 1920, Cohen became the rabbi of the congregation of Beth Shalom, in Philadelphia. As the years passed, the members of the congregation began moving to the suburbs and Cohen saw that it would soon be necessary for the synagogue itself to move. In the early nineteen-fifties land was purchased in Elkins Park and the congregation began to raise money for a new synagogue. Elated, Cohen set down on paper, in precise detail, his notion of what an ideal synagogue should be.

(3)   First of all, Cohen didn't want a building in the styles—**Gothic, Moorish,** and the like—that architects had used in the recent past. Secondly, he wanted his synagogue to take its inspiration from Mount Sinai, where, according to Jewish history, God had instructed Moses to build a tabernacle for the wandering Israelites. Jewish historians had written that "The Tabernacle is a moving Sinai," and Cohen decided that his new temple must somehow embody that image.

(4)   Cohen was convinced that Wright was the only man in the world who would be able to transform his ideas into reality, so, in 1953 Cohen sent Wright a letter:

> Dear Mr. Wright:
> . . . There is a dream and hope in my heart, of erecting a Synagogue that will be an inspiration for generations to come, so that people will come from all over the country to see it and find here a "new thing"—the dynamic American spirit joined with the ancient spirit of Israel . . . I am especially thrilled to feel that we shall have the opportunity of bringing your gifts into Philadelphia, the cradle of our democratic way of life.

(5)   The Rabbi added a PS: "On separate sheets, I explain my own philosophy of the synagogue that I would like to see created . . . I have also made a rudimentary sketch of its interior." Ordinarily, Wright ignored anyone who presumed to send him a sketch, but the letter was so obviously sincere and the sketch was so obviously remarkable that Wright replied, and set a date for a meeting with the Rabbi, on December 3, 1953.

Now, answer the questions that follow.

1. Elkins Park was an *affluent* suburb. What can you infer about the

   people who lived there? _____

Gothic: a style of architecture developed in northern France, which was popular in Europe from the middle of the 12th century until the early 16th century
Moorish: a style of architecture developed by the Arabs and Berbers who ruled southern Spain from the 8th to 14th centuries

188 / Unit 9

2. The fact that Frank Lloyd Wright and Mortimer Cohen worked together on the design was _____ because _____.

3. Cohen wanted the design of the new synagogue to _____
   Mount Sinai. Why do you think he chose this type of design?

   _____

4. Cohen hoped that the synagogue would _____ of America
   and the _____ of Israel. He also felt that Frank Lloyd Wright
   was _____.

5. What is the city of Philadelphia famous for? _____.

The Beth Shalom Synagogue—Part 2

(1)   In March 1954, Wright had completed seven sketches for the Synagogue. (To Cohen's delight, these were the sketches that bore his name as
co-designer.) The plans and elevations revealed that Wright had been able
to make an impressive structure out of Cohen's desire for "a mountain of
light, a moving Sinai." One of the definitions of the word *tabernacle* is "tent,"
and Wright had designed a shape that could be seen as either tent-like or
mountain-like. Three huge steel-and-concrete vertical supports rising a hundred and ten feet into the air formed a tripod from which hung sloping walls
of almost transparent plastic; these walls were divided into panels that gave
the approximately **hexagonal** exterior many pleasing surfaces, like the folds
in a curtain. The tripod itself rested on a base of reinforced concrete, from
which three wings emerged at a reverse angle to absorb the outward thrust
of the legs of the tripod. The small main entrance faced the street under a
canopy.

(2)   In the interior, a ground-level lobby gave access downward to a two-
hundred-and-fifty-seat chapel, two lounges (one of which was connected by
a sheltered passageway to the nearby school and community center), and
bathroom facilities, and upward, by twin flights of stairs to the left and right
of the entrance, into the main auditorium. The steps of the curving flights
of stairs were broad and deep and easy to climb. Visitors making their way

hexagonal: a shape having six sides

up the stairs from the lobby into the auditorium would encounter an optical surprise: they would be entering into the very heart of a mountain of light.

(3)   When one approaches the building from the outside, it is an impressive feat of technology, carried out in materials—concrete, aluminum, and industrial glass—that lack richness and refinement. But when we enter the **modest** lobby of Beth Shalom the building ceases to **intimidate** us. The rigid heaviness of the exterior changes to something quite different: magic spaces that seem to have no walls invite us simultaneously in and down and up and across. We feel **disoriented.** The floor of the auditorium floats under and around us like an immense, shallow dish, over which rises a pyramid that continuously brightens and darkens according to the amount of light that is available outside. Walking from one side of the auditorium to another, we cannot be sure whether we are ascending or descending. We are in an open space which has the feeling of a maze. We are only where we are, in the presence of a Presence.

Now, answer the questions that follow.

1. What does the word *tabernacle* mean? What was the overall shape of the outside of the temple?_____

2. What supported the outside walls of the temple? How many supports were there? _____

3. What was the geometric shape of the exterior of the temple? How many sides does this kind of shape have? _____

4. Think about the base of the building—what did the tripod rest on? What came up from the base? _____

5. Imagine that you are looking at the inside of the auditorium. What is the inside of the auditorium shaped like? _____

Exercise 11: Reading

Read a biographical account of an architect who interests you. (Suggestions: Aalto Alvar, Antonio Gaudí, Walter Gropius, Charles-Édouard Jeanneret (Le Corbusier), Maya Lin, Mies van der Rohe, Isamu Noguchi, I. M. Pei.)

modest: not bold; simple and quiet
to intimidate: to frighten someone; to make someone afraid
disoriented: confused; losing a sense of time, place, or identity

Or read about a famous building or another piece of architecture that you like. Consult recent encyclopedia yearbooks, library catalogs, and periodicals or ask the reference librarian for help. You may also want to look on the Internet by using a web browser like "InfoSeek." Be prepared to give a three- to five-minute presentation to the class based on your reading. It may be helpful and interesting to incorporate photos or drawings of the architect and his or her work in your presentation.

Exercise 12: Speaking

Use the following questions to interview another student about the architect or building he or she researched for Exercise 11.

For an architect

1. Who is the architect?
2. How did he or she get interested or started in architecture?
3. What is distinctive about his or her work?
4. What are some of his or her major accomplishments?
5. Where have his or her works been built?
6. What awards has he or she won?

For a building or piece of architecture

1. What is the name of the building? Where is it? When was it built?
2. Who built it? What other buildings is this person known for?
3. Does this building have a special purpose or function? Was it built for any special reason?
4. What do you feel is distinctive or unusual about this building?
5. What materials is the building made of?
6. Why did you select this piece of architecture?

Exercise 13: Writing

Write a short report about the architect or building that you researched for Exercise 11. Be sure to answer the appropriate questions from Exercise 12 in your report and include illustrations or photos if possible.

Review Unit 3

I. Choose the correct word from the list on the left to go with each meaning. (In each set, you will not use two of the words.)

Set A

1. intimate   __ decrease
2. integration   __ union
3. capacity   __ capability
4. subside
5. constitution

Set B

1. imperial   __ calculation
2. estimation   __ royal
3. monarch   __ concurrent
4. simultaneous
5. focus

Set C

1. deprive   __ disprove
2. distort   __ use
3. extract   __ pull out
4. refute
5. utilize

II. Identify the following words as synonyms (*S*) or antonyms (*A*).

   __ 1. release/liberate   __ 5. conclude/commence
   __ 2. evaporate/condense   __ 6. oscillate/fluctuate
   __ 3. inferior/lesser   __ 7. integrate/segregate
   __ 4. diverge/branch off   __ 8. revive/kill

III. Match each word on the left with a word on the right with which it often collocates.

     __ 1. military   a. rooms

     __ 2. constitutional   b. quality

     __ 3. data   c. statement

     __ 4. inferior   d. formula

     __ 5. adjacent   e. destiny

     __ 6. traditional   f. rights

     __ 7. concluding   g. analysis

     __ 8. manifest   h. intuition

                                i. academy

                                j. values

IV. Write the name of the currency or the system of money used in each country.

    1. Argentina   _____

    2. Italy   _____

    3. Germany   _____

    4. Great Britain   _____

    5. France   _____

    6. Mexico   _____

V. Given the Spanish you have learned, what do the following words mean?

    1. Santa Clara pueblo = Santa Clara _____

    2. adobe dwelling   = _____ dwelling

    3. chile con carne   = _____ with meat

    4. Rio Bravo   = Raging _____

    5. chile relleno   = stuffed _____

    6. Rio de la Plata   = _____ of Silver

VI. Complete each sentence with one of the words given here.

texture   focus   lenses

motives   constructs   attached

1. A florist _____ a corsage from the heads of flowers.

2. The city is usually a major _____ of river, railway, and road connections.

3. Some _____ such as hunger and thirst are best under-stood from a biological perspective.

4. The surface _____ of the earth varies from fine sand to coarse gravel.

5. Contact _____ , worn on the surface of the eyes, are commonly used to correct defects of vision.

6. The rabbi _____ his drawings for the synagogue to the letter he sent Wright.

University Word List Index

This list, compiled by Xue and Nation (1984), contains approximately 800 words that students need to know in order to read college-level texts. Words studied in this text, *More Mastery,* are set in bold-faced type and marked by the number of the unit and page number on which they appear. Words studied in *Mastery* (book 1) are marked with "1" and the number of the unit in which they appear. Words in the Academic Word List (1998) that do not appear in the University Word List follow after the University Word List.

A
abandon
abnormal
absorb (1:11)
abstract (abstraction) (1:7)
academic (academically) (6:115)
accelerate
access
accompany
accomplish (1:3)
accumulate (3:49)
accurate (accuracy) (1:11)
achieve
acid
acquire
adapt (1:1)
adequate
adhere
adjacent (9:179)
adjective
adjust (adjustments) (1:2)
administer
adolescent
adult
advocate
aesthetic
affiliate
affluence (affluent) (6:115)
aggregate
aggression

agitate
aid
alcohol (1:6)
align (5:95)
allege
allocate
allude
ally (allied) (1:9)
alter
alternative (1:11)
ambiguity
amorphous
analogy
analyze
angular
annual
anomaly
anonymous
anthropology (5:95)
apparatus
appeal
append
appendix
appraise
appreciate
approach (1:3)
appropriate (1:2)
approximate (approximately) (1:11)
arbitrary (1:4)
area

aristocrat
arithmetic
arouse
ascribe
aspect (7:137)
aspiration
assemble (assembly) (1:1)
assent
assert
assess
asset (2:30)
assign (1:4)
assimilate
assist (1:5)
assume
assure (1:11)
astronomy
atmosphere (1:11)
atom
attach (7:137)
attain (1:5)
attitude
attribute (3:49)
auspices
authorize (authorities) (2:30)
automatic (1:1)
avail (available) (1:1)
averse
aware (1:9)
awe
axis

define
definite
deflect (deflection) (9:179)
degenerate
degrade
deliberate (deliberately) (2:30)
democracy (Democrats) (4:75)
demonstrate
denominator
denote
dense
deny
depress (depression) (1:6)
deprive (8:156)
derive
design (1:7)
detect
detriment (detrimental) (2:30)
deviate (deviation) (4:75)
devise
devote (devotion) (1:9)
diagram (1:8)
diameter (1:2)
dictate
diffuse (8:156)
digest
dimension
discern (2:30)
discourse
discrete (6:115)
dispense
disperse
displace
dispose
dispute
dissipate
dissolve
distinct (distinction) (5:95)
distort (distortion) (9:179)
distribute
diverge (divergent) (8:156)
diverse (5:95)
divine
doctrine (8:156)

domestic
dominate
drain (3:49)
drama (1:4)
drastic
drug (1:6)
duration
dynamic

E
economy (1:1)
edit (1:6)
efficient
elaborate (2:30)
electron
element (1:7)
elevate (elevation) (3:49)
elicit
eliminate (1:5)
eloquent (1:9)
emancipate
embody
embrace (1:3)
emerge (1:3)
emotion (1:3)
emphasize (1:11)
empirical
enable
energy (3:49)
enhance
enlighten
enrich (1:7)
ensure
entity
enumerate
environment (1:8)
episode (2:30)
equate
equidistant
equilibrium
equipment
equivalent
err
establish (1:5)
estimate (7:137)
ethics
evaluate

evaporate (7:137)
eventual (eventually) (5:95)
evident (1:3)
evoke (1:2)
evolve (1:6)
exclude (exclusive) (6:115)
execute (executive) (4:75)
exert
exhaust
expand
expel
expert (1:9)
explicit
exploit
exponent (1:5)
export
expose (2:30)
external
extract (7:137)

F
facilitate
faction
factor
fallacy
fare
fate
feasible
feature (1:1)
federal
fertile (1:7)
final
finance (financially) (1:6)
finite
fluctuate
fluent (6:115)
fluid
focus (8:156)
forego
formulate
fossil
found (7:137)
fraction
fragment (5:95)
frantic (7:137)
fraternal
fraud

R
radiant
radius
random
range
ratio
rational
react (reaction) (1:8)
rebel
rectangle (1:7)
recur
reform
refute (8:156)
region
reign
reinforce (9:179)
reject
release (7:137)
relevance
reluctant
rely (reliable) (1:9)
remove
render
repress
repudiate
require (8:156)
research (1:1)
reservoir
resident (reside) (1:4)
residue
resource
respective
respond (response) (2:30)
restore
restrict
retain
retard
reveal (1:7)
reverberate
reverse (1:6)
revise
revive (9:179)
revolt (1:4)
revolve
rhythm (1:11)
rigid
rigor (rigourous) (1:9)

role (4:75)
rotate (1:4)
route (3:49)
rudimentary
rural

S
saint
sanction
satellite
saturate
scalar
schedule
scheme
score
secrete
section
secure (1:11)
seek
segment
select
sequence
series (1:3)
sex (6:115)
shift (1:11)
shrink (1:11)
sibling
signify
similar (3:49)
**simultaneous (simultane-
    ously) (7:137)**
site (1:2)
skeleton
sketch (1:7)
sociology (1:5)
solar (1:8)
sophisticated
source
spatial
species
specify (specific) (1:2)
spectrum
**speculate (speculation)
    (6:115)**
sphere
spontaneous
stable

starve
stationary
statistic (1:3)
status (6:115)
stereotype
stimulate
stipulate
strata
stress (stressful) (1:11)
structure
style (stylized) (5:95)
subdivide
subjective
subordinate
subsequent
subside (9:179)
subsidize
subtle
suffice
sum
summary
superficial
superimpose
superior (1:7)
supplement (1:3)
suppress
supreme (1:2)
surplus
survey (3:49)
suspend
sustain
switch
**symbol (symbolic)
    (6:115)**
symptom
synthetic

T
tangent
tangible
tape
task (1:9)
team (1:9)
technique (5:95)
technology (1:8)
telescope
temporary

tense (tension) (1:11)
tentative
terminology
territory
terror (1:3)
text (1:2)
texture (9:179)
theft
theorem
theory (1:7)
thermal
tiny (1:6)
tire
tissue
tolerate
tone
topic
trace
tractor
tradition (traditional)
  (7:137)
traffic
trait
transact
transfer

transform (transformation)
  (1:6)
transition
transmit
transparent
transport
treaty
trend
triangle
trivial
tropical

U
ultimate (ultimately)
  (4:75)
undergo
underlie
undertake (1:5)
unduly
uniform
upsurge
urban (1:5)
usage
utilize (utilities) (9:179)
utter (1:3)

V
vague
valid
vary
vast
vein
velocity
verbal
verify (4:75)
version (1:1)
vertical (vertically) (5:95)
vibrate
violate (violation) (6:115)
virtual
visual (visualize) (1:7)
vital
vocabulary
volt
volume
voluntary (volunteer) (1:5)

W
withdraw (1:3)

X
X-ray

Words on the Academic Word List (1998) that do not appear on the University Word List (1984)

A
accommodate
acknowledge
affect
albeit
amend
anticipate
apparent
author
authority
available

B
behalf
bias
bond
brief

C
chart
cite
civil
clause
coherent
colleague
commence
commission
community
compatible
compile
comprehensive
concurrent
confirm
considerable
constrain

contemporary
convince
core
couple
criteria

D
deduce
despite
device
differentiate
diminish
discriminate
display
document
domain
draft

Answer Key

Unit 1: Billie Jean King

Vocabulary Preview

Preview 1 (p. 2)
1. rhythm
2. accuracy
3. atmosphere
4. stressful
5. injury

Preview 2 (p. 2)
1. c
2. e
3. d
4. a
5. b

Reading Preview (p. 3)
1. d
2. c
3. a

Comprehension Check (p. 9)
1. F
2. T
3. F
4. F
5. T
6. T
7. T
8. F

Critical Thinking (p. 9)
1. got into routine of staying up late and sleeping until ten or eleven in the morning, lifted weights to strengthen legs and knees, got a lot of rest, played twice a day with Pete Collins, rallied a lot, tried to get a good rhythm going, hit to see how long they could keep the ball in play, practiced volleying, practiced changing her service around, practiced hitting to backhand side and then hitting sharply to forehand side, got up late and ate breakfast, ate candy all day, went to the Astrodome to get the feel of the court, practiced hitting on the Astrodome court
2. self answers should include the following: got into routine of staying up late and sleeping until ten or eleven in the morning, lifted weights to strengthen legs and knees, got a lot of rest, got up late and ate breakfast, ate candy all day game answers should include the following: played twice a day with Pete Collins, rallied a lot, tried to get a good rhythm going, hit to see how long they could keep the ball in play, practiced volleying, practiced changing her service around, practiced hitting to backhand side and then hitting sharply to forehand side, went to the Astrodome to get the feel of the court, practiced hitting on the Astrodome court
3. Answers will vary.

Exercise 1 (p. 11)
A.
1. conservative
2. nervous
3. injurious
4. analogous
5. alternative
6. definitive

B.
1. nervous
2. Alternative
3. analogous
4. conservative
5. definitive
6. injurious

Exercise 2 (p. 12)
1. exact
2. ignore
3. carelessness
4. speed
5. dangerous
6. selection

Exercise 3 (p. 13)
1. solid : earth :: gas : <u>atmosphere, oxygen</u>
2. mind : mental :: body : <u>physical</u>
3. give off : secrete :: take in : <u>absorb</u>
4. unique : distinct :: different : <u>alternative</u>
5. square : cube :: circle : <u>cylinder</u>
6. cover : expose :: lower : <u>elevate</u>

Exercise 4 (p. 14)
1. A, 2 reason: referring to gears
2. C reason: scheduled period of work
3. A, 1 reason: moved from place to place
4. B, 1 reason: a dress
5. A, 1 reason: change position

Exercise 5 (p. 14)
1. interviewer
2. emphatic
3. absorbent
4. approximately
5. precisely

Exercise 6 (p. 15)
1. b
2. a
3. c
4. b
5. c
6. a

Exercise 7 (p. 16)
1. alternative
2. shift
3. atmosphere
4. interview
5. conservatively
6. physical

Exercise 8 (p. 16)
1. What was Billie Jean's routine when she played tennis at night?
2. What was Billie Jean's alternative game strategy?
3. Why are precision and accuracy (*or* accuracy and precision) needed in tennis?
4. Why was the hour before the match so stressful for Billie Jean?
5. Who emphasized the ten-minute injury time-out?
6. Do you think the match was harder physically or mentally?

Exercise 9 (p. 17)
1. I was <u>kind</u> of <u>shocked</u> because I thought he would be a lot better than he was. He didn't have a big service, and his spins <u>weren't</u> <u>that</u> <u>great</u> either.
2. And I was <u>absolutely</u> <u>right</u> about him not <u>realizing</u> how quick I was at the net or how well I could volley.
3. I <u>concentrated</u> <u>hard</u> on winning that first set and when I did I knew he was in big trouble. That meant he would have to play <u>at</u> <u>least</u> four tough sets to win the match, prob-ably more hard <u>competitive</u> tennis than he'd played in years.
4. I felt I was in pretty <u>good</u> <u>shape,</u> and that things were going <u>my</u> way.

Exercise 10 (p. 17)
Answers will vary.

Exercise 11 (p. 18)
Answers will vary.

Exercise 12 (p. 18)
Answers will vary.

Unit 2: Nien Cheng

Vocabulary Preview

Preview 1 (p. 20)
1. inhibited
2. episode
3. confined
4. assets
5. policy

Preview 2 (p. 20)
1. d
2. a
3. e
4. c
5. b

Reading Preview (p. 21)
1. a
2. b
3. c

Comprehension Check (p. 28)
1. F
2. F
3. F
4. F
5. T
6. T
7. T
8. T
9. T
10. F

Critical Thinking (p. 28)

Answers will vary, but should include the following.
1. Mao's policies had a harmful effect on human relationships. People didn't speak openly to each other or trust one another. People no longer wanted to have friends. They kept their thoughts to themselves or lied in order to protect themselves and their families.
2. In the reading, Cheng was accused of being a spy because she supposedly had her picture taken with her brothers in front of the Sun Yatsen Memorial. The introduction to the reading mentions that her husband had been a diplomat for the Kuomintang government and they had both worked for a foreign oil company.
3. The clothes in the bundle looked new and clean, as though they had not been used. Also, Meiping's teacup was dirty, as though something had suddenly happened to her and she had not had time to wash it.

Exercise 1 (p. 30)
pro- means *for* or *in support of*
anti- means *against* or *opposed to*
1. antiwar
2. antitrust
3. pro-family
4. Antifreeze
5. Proabortion
6. pro-American

Exercise 2 (p. 31)
1. confinement
2. discernment
3. assessment
4. achievement
5. investment

Exercise 3 (p. 32)
1. c
2. e
3. a
4. f
5. b
6. d

Exercise 4 (p. 33)
Synonyms will differ, but examples are given.
1. d   goods
2. f   purposeful
3. a   intricate
4. e   show
5. b   fear
6. h   prevent

7. c   cloth
8. g   rule

Exercise 5 (p. 33)
1. monetary assets, government assets
2. deliberate choice, deliberate lie
3. elaborate story, elaborate lie
4. horror movie, horror story
5. obvious choice, obvious lie
6. government policy, monetary policy

Exercise 6 (p. 34)
1. authorized
2. discernible
3. exposure
4. horrible
5. materialistic
6. responded

Exercise 7 (p. 35)
1. inhibited
2. intelligent
3. obviously
4. response
5. confined
6. deliberately
7. occurred
8. terrible

Exercise 8 (p. 35)
1. a
2. c
3. c
4. a

Exercise 9 (p. 36)
1. assert
2. cell
3. confine
4. design
5. expose
6. error
7. intense
8. occur

Exercise 10 (p. 36)
Answers will vary.

Exercise 11 (p. 37)
Answers will vary.

Exercise 12 (p. 38)
Answers will vary.

Unit 3: Jon Krakauer

Vocabulary Preview

Preview 1 (p. 40)
1. process
2. elevation
3. accumulated
4. maintain
5. survey

Preview 2 (p. 40)
1. c
2. e
3. b
4. a
5. d

Reading Preview (p. 41)

1. d
2. c
3. d

Comprehension Check (p. 47)

1. F
2. F
3. T
4. T
5. T
6. T
7. F
8. F

Critical Thinking (p. 47)

1. Answers will vary.
2. Answers will vary.
3. Answers will vary. There are many disadvantages to having inexperienced climbers on an expedition. They are often less physically fit; they may make poor decisions because of their inexperience; they may put other climbers in danger with their poor decisions or actions; they may need to be rescued, and this puts more climbers in danger.

Exercise 1 (p. 49)
deactivate, decaffeinated, deplane, devalue
1. c
2. a
3. d
4. b
disapprove, disintegrate, disorient, displace
5. c
6. b
7. d
8. a

Exercise 2 (p. 50)
1. decaffeinated
2. displaced
3. disoriented
4. deplane
5. devalue
6. disapprove
7. deactivate
8. disintegrate

Exercise 3 (p. 51)
alliance, assurance, conference, divergence, occurrence, maintenance, persistence, reliance
1. maintenance
2. conference
3. persistence
4. divergence
5. occurrence
6. reliance
7. alliance
8. assurance
Possible answers are as follows: insurance, correspondence, affluence

Exercise 4 (p. 52)
1. A
2. A
3. S
4. S
5. S
6. A
7. S
8. A

Exercise 5 (p. 52)
1. C
2. I   Experienced climbers have
           accumulated
      ~~elevated~~ a lot of knowledge
                ^
      about proper climbing tech-
      niques, safety, and first aid.
3. I   Stress and fatigue can cause
           elevated
      ~~accumulated~~ blood pressure.
                ^
4. C
5. C
6. I   Public buildings are required to
              elevators
      have ~~elevates~~ that can be used
                 ^
      easily by disabled persons.

Exercise 6 (p. 53)
1. b
2. b
3. a
4. c
5. b

Exercise 7 (p. 54)
Answers will vary.

Exercise 8 (p. 55)
1. pliant
2. debate
3. bowl
4. neighbor
5. context
6. rain
7. previous
8. route
9. dress
10. schemes

Exercise 9 (p. 55)
Answers will vary.

Exercise 10 (p. 56)
Extreme sports, such as skateboarding, snowboarding, in-line skating, bicycle stunt riding, and rock climbing, are

increasingly popular with young Americans. In cities across the country, <u>energetic</u> young men and women can be seen carrying skateboards or strapping on knee pads and roller blades and heading to the nearest skate park.

Skateboarding is perhaps the most popular extreme sport among an important group of consumers: young American males. Advertisers have <u>responded</u> to this popularity, and skateboarders now appear in ads for everything from snack foods to telephone services. Skateboarding is so popular that many communities have built their own skate parks. The city of Escondido, California, recently opened a two million dollar sports center that features an <u>elaborate</u> 20,000 foot skate park—the largest in the country. Skate parks are growing increasingly sophisticated, too, with a variety of <u>inclines,</u> <u>elevated</u> ramps, pipes, and bowls designed to test even the best skateboarders.

Snowboarding is <u>similar</u> to skateboarding in that participants do stunts with a flat board, but a snowboard has no wheels. Snowboarding also requires one thing that skateboarding does not: snow. Many serious athletes actually participate in both sports, and there are a number of "tricks" or moves that can be done on either type of board. Some snowboard moves are also taken from downhill skiing: the giant slalom and "big air" jumping are two examples. However, compared to skateboarding and skiing, snowboarding can be a very risky sport. More than one young athlete has had his or her snowboarding career ended by a severe <u>injury</u> or death.

So, what makes these <u>physically</u> demanding sports so appealing? Why are young people <u>shifting</u> away from more <u>conservative,</u> traditional sports to these risky <u>alternative</u> sports? A survey of

young X-tremers, as they call themselves, may give us some insight. Most love extreme sports because they are challenging and exciting. These sports <u>expose</u> the participants to risk, and only those athletes with physical strength, coordination, balance, timing, luck, and nerves of steel can meet the challenge. Do these sound like <u>attributes</u> that you have? If so, maybe you should give an extreme sport a try. But please be careful!

1. Several extreme sports are skateboarding, snowboarding, in-line skating, bicycle stunt riding, and rock climbing. Skateboarding is the most popular.
2. Advertisers now use skateboarders to advertise all types of products, and many communities have built skate parks.
3. According to the article, snowboarding is the most dangerous of the extreme sports. Personal opinions will vary.
4. Personal opinions will vary.

Exercise 11 (p. 57)
Answers will vary.

Review Unit 1

I. (p. 58)
Set A: 4, 5, 2
Set B: 5, 2, 1
Set C: 4, 1, 3

II. (p. 59)
1. S
2. A
3. S
4. A
5. S
6. S
7. A
8. A

III. (p. 59)
1. i
2. f

3. e
4. j
5. d
6. c
7. h
8. b

IV. (p. 59)
1. assured
2. authorities
3. discern
4. occurrence
5. materialistic
6. elevation

V. (p. 60)
1. impulse
2. cell
3. intense
4. rhythm
5. cylinder
6. survey

VI. (p. 60)
1. oxygen
2. episodes
3. accuracy
4. attribute
5. atmosphere
6. energy

Unit 4: Katharine Graham

Vocabulary Preview

Preview 1 (p. 63)
1. executive
2. investigating
3. crisis
4. comments
5. journalism

Preview 2 (p. 63)
1. b
2. d
3. e
4. c
5. a

Reading Preview (p. 64)

Answers will vary.

Comprehension Check (p. 73)
1. F
2. F
3. F
4. T
5. T
6. F
7. F
8. T

Critical Thinking (p. 74)

Answers will vary.

Exercise 1 (p. 75)
1. a marriage between people of different races (*Example:* black and white)
2. a religious service attended by people from different religious faiths (*Example:* Christians and Buddhists)
3. a video game that is played by manipulating a remote control
4. a parent stepping in to stop or mediate the argument
5. a place where two roads cross each other
6. two different galaxies, or representatives of two different galaxies, interacting, colliding, or intersecting

Exercise 2 (p. 76)
1. a
2. b
3. c
4. c
5. a

Exercise 3 (p. 77)
1. unthinkable
2. doubtful
3. book
4. falsify
5. conform
6. monarchy

Exercise 4 (p. 77)
1. R
2. C
3. R
4. C
5. R

Exercise 5 (p. 78)

Noun	Noun (person)	Adjective	Adverb	Verb
execution	executor	executable	—	execute
democracy	democrat	democratic	democratically	democratize
contribution	contributor	contributive, contributory	contributively	contribute
investigation	investigator	investigative, investigatory, investigational	—	investigate
journalism, journal	journalist	journalistic	journalistically	journalize
commentary, comment	commentator	—	—	comment
credibility	—	credible	credibly	—

Exercise 6 (p. 79)
1. executor
2. credibility
3. investigative
4. commentary
5. Democratic
6. contributors

Exercise 7 (p. 79)
1. circle: to look everywhere for hard evidence
   Type of clue: brief definition
2. circle: That is, newspapers, magazines, radio, and television are at liberty to disclose any story about events or people
   Type of clue: direct explanation
3. circle: the field of producing, gathering, and reporting news for the media
   Type of clue: brief definition
4. circle: as long as they are legal, as long as they don't break any laws
   Type of clue: contrast
5. circle: The editors had made up their minds to handle the story with more than the usual exacting, precise attention to fairness and detail.
   Type of clue: direct explanation
6. circle: The paper became known throughout the world because of it.
   Type of clue: direct explanation

Exercise 8 (p. 80)
1. a
2. b
3. b
4. c
5. a
6. b

Exercise 9 (p. 82)
1. White House counsel (Reading Preview)
2. Former attorney general and head of the Nixon reelection campaign (Reading Preview)
3. Nixon's chief of staff (Reading Preview)
4. special prosecutor (Reading Preview)
5. Nixon's secretary of commerce (7)
6. judge (14)

Exercise 10 (p. 82)
1. to gather intelligence information on the Democrats
2. that he was one of the other four people authorized to approve payments from the secret fund
3. John Dean, his counsel
4. editorial lunches held at the *Post*
5. It was sent to Haldeman in a memo.
6. television stations

Exercise 11 (p. 83)
1. (Other newspapers did not) jump on it (the Watergate story): Other newspapers did not immediately start writing about it. (5)
2. (The *Post* did not want to be) set up: The paper did not want to be tricked into publishing a story that was not true. (9)
3. (We paid) a large price: Yes, many good things happened to the *Post* because of Watergate, but also, there were many long-lasting negative consequences. (13)
4. (The way the *Post* handled the story) stood the test of time: Looking back, twenty-five years later, the *Post* could still say it had acted properly in covering Watergate. (17)

Exercise 12 (p. 83)
Answers will vary.

Exercise 13 (p. 84)
Answers will vary.

Exercise 14 (p. 84)
Answers will vary.

Unit 5: María Martínez

Vocabulary Preview

Preview 1 (p. 86)
1. aligned
2. indigenous
3. fragments
4. diverse
5. carbonize

Preview 2 (p. 86)
1. d
2. a
3. e
4. c
5. b

Reading Preview (p. 87)
Answers will vary.

Comprehension Check (p. 93)
1. T
2. T
3. F
4. F
5. F
6. F
7. F
8. T

Critical Thinking (p. 93)
Answers will vary.

Exercise 1 (p. 95)
1. d
2. c
3. a
4. e
5. b
6. f

Exercise 2 (p. 95)
1. prevent
2. precedent
3. precedes
4. presupposes
5. preliminary
6. premature

Exercise 3 (p. 96)
Answers will vary.

Exercise 4 (p. 96)
Antonyms will vary but may include the following.

Word	Antonym
1. vertical	horizontal
2. precede	follow
3. eventual	current

4. fragments   whole
5. indigenous   foreign
6. intuitive   thoughtful

Exercise 5 (p. 97)
1. originally
2. usually
3. eventually
4. habitually
5. ultimately
6. finally

Exercise 6 (p. 97)
1. wooden   Adj
2. offender   N
3. made   V
4. named   V
5. understand   V
6. years   N

Exercise 7 (p. 98)
1. b
2. a
3. e
4. c
5. d

Exercise 8 (p. 99)

(1) Carbon, a nonmetallic chemical element, exists in three forms. Two of the forms are diamond and graphite. Pure diamond is the hardest naturally occurring substance known and is a poor conductor of electricity. Graphite, on the other hand, is a soft, slippery solid that is a good conductor of both heat and electricity. Because of their beauty, diamonds are valued as jewels, and because of their hardness, they are valued for cutting, grinding, and drilling.

(2) The third form of carbon, known as carbon black, is amorphous, meaning that it lacks a definite form. Included in carbon black are charcoal, coke, and coal. All forms of carbon black are products of oxidation, that is, of uniting with oxygen. Oxidation occurs in burning or rusting and in other forms of decomposition of organic compounds. Carbon black has many uses. In addition to being used extensively as fuel, it is also used to make ink, typewriter ribbons, and carbon paper.

(3) Carbon combines and links easily with other atoms to form over a million carbon compounds. In fact, carbon's compounds are so numerous, complex, and important that their study constitutes a specialized field of chemistry called organic chemistry. The field of organic chemistry derives its name from the fact that, in the nineteenth century, most of the then-known carbon compounds were considered to have originated in living organisms.

1. diamonds, graphite, coal
2. Diamonds are valued for their beauty and their hardness.
3. Most of the carbon compounds known in the nineteenth century were believed to have come from living (organic) things.

Exercise 9 (p. 100)
1. b
2. c
3. a
4. c
5. b

Exercise 10 (p. 101)
1. b
2. a
3. a
4. c
5. d
6. c
7. a
8. b

Exercise 11 (p. 101)
1. b
2. c
3. a
4. c
5. b

Exercise 12 (p. 102)
Answers will vary but should contain the following information.
1. black-on-black pottery
2. in the ruins around San Ildefonso
3. decoration
4. burnishing or polishing the pot, painting on the design, and, finally, smothering the kiln fire with manure to carbonize the clay
5. water serpents
6. carried by hand or brought in a truck
7. by 46-ounce tomato cans
8. in New Mexico, in the Southwest

Exercise 13 (p. 103)
Answers will vary.

Exercise 14 (p. 103)
Answers will vary.

Exercise 15 (p. 103)
Pueblo Indian Culture
1. *Anthropological* means related to the customs and culture of a group of people—in this case, the customs and cultures of the Pueblo Indians. Many centuries before European explorers found their way to the Western Hemisphere, the Pueblo Indians of what is now New Mexico developed a distinctive civilization. These peace-loving people created an urban life in harmony with the environment, and they also lived in harmony with each other. Their religion was deeply spiritual and con-stituted an important part of their daily life within which they created highly developed art, especially in pottery, weaving, jewelry, textiles, and leatherwork.
2. *Distinctive* means unique or notable. Distinctive about San Ildefonso is the famous black-on-black pottery manufactured there. The making of this black-on-black pottery was re-vived primarily because of María Martínez. Today these pots com-mand worldwide the respect of collectors of fine art.
3. *Preceded* means come before. The Pueblo Indians preceded European explorers by many centuries.

The Making of Traditional Tewa Pottery
1. *Distinctive* means unique, special, or unusual. The raw materials must be available from tribal lands. They should be purified manually, prefer-ably by the potter or close members of the potter's family.
2. *Technique* means method or process. The ware must be formed and fin-ished by hand methods such as coiling or pinching. The use of the potter's wheel or plaster molds is frowned upon by the classic Tewa potter.
3. *Fuel* refers to the wood or manure burned to heat the kiln. The work must be fired in temporary kilns built on the spot at the time of each individual firing, using only wood or manure as fuel. Firing in com-mercially available kilns heated with secondary fuel such as oil or electricity is considered an especially poor practice.

Unit 6: Madeleine Albright

Vocabulary Preview

Preview 1 (p. 107)
1. frustrated
2. linguist
3. affluent
4. constantly
5. academically

Preview 2 (p. 107)
1. d
2. a
3. e
4. b
5. c

Reading Preview (p. 108)

1. c
2. d
3. a

Comprehension Check (p. 114)

1. T
2. F
3. T
4. F
5. F
6. T
7. T
8. T

Critical Thinking (p. 114)

1. The Korbels lived in comfortable, sometimes luxurious quarters and had help to take care of daily cooking and cleaning.
2. Answers will vary but may include the following. The Korbels had a less affluent life. Mrs. Korbel did their cooking and cleaning. They did not have a car or a television. They may not have had much money, because Madeleine's clothes were often too big or too small.
3. Answers will vary but may include the following. Madeleine's father was a diplomat who spoke several lan-guages. Madeleine lived and went to school in several different countries as a child.
4. Answers will vary.

Exercise 1 (p. 115)
inconclusive, inconstant, discredit, dis-inclined, immaterial, imprecise, inse-cure, dissimilar
1. disinclined
2. imprecise
3. insecure
4. inconclusive
5. dissimilar
6. discredit
7. immaterial
8. inconstant

Exercise 2 (p. 116)
1. refutable
2. verifiable
3. discernible
4. attributable
5. maintainable

Exercise 3 (p. 116)
1. bureaucratic
2. mythic
3. academic
4. Strategic
5. democratic

Exercise 4 (p. 117)
1. c, k
2. a, j
3. b, g
4. d, h
5. f, l
6. e, i
Synonyms will vary.

Exercise 5 (p. 117)
1. academic accomplishment, academic report, academic policy
2. bureaucratic policy, bureaucratic report, bureaucratic scandal
3. constant attention, constant value
4. discrete point, discrete value
5. major scandal, major value
6. sex appeal, sex scandal, sex symbol

Exercise 6 (p. 118)

Noun	Noun (person)	Adjective	Adverb	Verb
academy	academic, academician	academic	academically	—
bureaucracy	bureaucrat	*bureaucratic*	bureaucratically	bureaucratize
invasion	*invader*	invasive	invasively	invade
prosperity	—	prosperous	prosperously	*prosper*
speculation	speculator	speculative	speculatively	speculate
frustration	—	*frustrated,* frustrating	frustratedly, frustratingly	frustrate

Exercise 7 (p. 119)
1. b
2. c
3. b
4. a
5. b
6. b

Exercise 8 (p. 120)
1. frustrated
2. major, prominent
3. speculation
4. status
5. sex
6. symbolic

Exercise 9 (p. 120)
1. b
2. a
3. b
4. c
5. a

Exercise 10 (p. 121)
Answers will vary.

Exercise 11 (p. 122)
1. b
2. c
3. b
4. a
5. c

Exercise 12 (p. 124)
Answers will vary.

Review Unit 2

I. (p. 125)
Set A: 4, 3, 5
Set B: 3, 5, 1
Set C: 5, 4, 2

II. (p. 125)
1. A
2. A
3. S
4. A
5. A
6. S
7. S
8. A

III. (p. 126)
1. i
2. d
3. b
4. g
5. h
6. a
7. j
8. f

IV. (p. 126)
1. inconstant
2. convention
3. dislocation
4. distinction
5. inviolate
6. verifiable

V. (p. 126)
1. democracy
2. distinct
3. vertical
4. fuel
5. major
6. intuition

VI. (p. 127)
1. circulate
2. convene
3. network
4. Linguistics
5. role
6. symbol

Unit 7: Ansel Adams

Vocabulary Preview

Preview 1 (p. 129)
1. found
2. evaporated
3. currency
4. computed
5. estimate

Preview 2 (p. 129)
1. e
2. a
3. d
4. b
5. c

Reading Preview (p. 130)

Answers will vary.

Comprehension Check (p. 135)
1. T
2. T
3. F
4. F
5. T
6. T
7. F
8. T

Critical Thinking (p. 136)

Answers will vary.

Exercise 1 (p. 137)
A.
1. perspective: the art of picturing objects so as to show relative distance or depth; sense of proportion; a specific point of view
2. perceive: to understand; to become aware of through the senses
3. perceptible: able to be seen or known through the senses
B.
1. perspective
2. perception
3. perceptible

Exercise 2 (p. 138)

Noun	Noun (person)	Adjective	Adverb	Verb
publication	publisher	published, publishable	—	publish
investment	investor	invested, investable	—	invest
foundation	founder	founded, foundational	foundationally	found
attachment	attaché	attached, attachable	—	attach
collection, collectible	collector	collectible collective	collectively	collect
photography	photographer	photographic	photographically	photograph

Exercise 3 (p. 138)

Tripod set up. Camera secured. Lens attached. Film inserted. However, no exposure meter for, in all the rush, it could not be found! Perhaps only Ansel Adams could have recalled under such pressure that the luminance of the full moon is 250 candles per square foot, and then calculated the exposure formula; his years of hard work and technical mastery of photography had readied him for this moment. (Ansel's favorite aphorism paraphrased Louis Pasteur: "Chance favors the prepared mind.")

Exercise 4 (p. 139)
Answers will vary.

Exercise 5 (p. 139)
1. d
2. c
3. c
4. a
5. e
6. b

Exercise 6 (p. 140)
1. Vestments
2. vestry
3. vest
4. invested
5. investiture

Exercise 7 (p. 140)
1. Japan
2. Korea
3. China
4. Germany
5. Peru
6. Russia
7. Israel
8. Venezuela
9. Ecuador
10. Poland

Exercise 8 (p. 141)
1. c
2. c
3. b

4. a
5. c
6. a

Exercise 9 (p. 143)
1. a
2. a
3. a
4. b
5. c
6. c

Exercise 10 (p. 144)
Answers will vary.

Exercise 11 (p. 145)
Answers will vary.

Exercise 12 (p. 145)
Answers will vary.

Exercise 13 (p. 146)
Answers will vary.

Unit 8: Thurgood Marshall

Vocabulary Preview

Preview 1 (p. 148)
1. liberal
2. data
3. capacity
4. diffuse
5. motivated

Preview 2 (p. 148)
1. c
2. a
3. e
4. b
5. d

Reading Preview (p. 149)

1. c
2. b
3. a

Comprehension Check (p. 155)

1. F
2. T
3. T
4. T

5. F
6. F
7. T
8. T

Critical Thinking (p. 155)

Answers will vary but may include the following.
1. Marshall was intelligent and well educated; he had a sense of humor; he was good at bringing together groups of people to share ideas and look at a situation from different perspectives; he was good at diffusing tensions; he was a good mimic; he was good at making people feel comfortable and share their ideas; he was good at synthesizing other people's ideas.
2. He smoked a lot; he got grumpy and snapped at his secretaries when he was overworked.

Exercise 1 (p. 156)
1. capture
2. caption
3. capable
4. captivate
5. captivity
6. capacity
7. captured
8. captive

Exercise 2 (p. 157)
1. liberate
2. liberator
3. Liberty
4. liberalize
5. liberals

Exercise 3 (p. 158)
1. disintegration
2. automobile
3. refund
4. unconstitutional
5. demobilized
6. irrefutable

Exercise 4 (p. 158)
A.
1. deprivation
2. diffusion
3. integration
4. conclusion
5. constitution
B.
1. deprived
2. conclusion
3. integration
4. conclude
5. integrate
6. diffused
7. constitution
8. constitutes
9. deprivation
10. diffusion

Exercise 5 (p. 159)
1. extrinsic
2. preferred
3. heresy
4. unite
5. endow
6. stationary

Exercise 6 (p. 160)
1. S
2. S
3. A
4. S
5. S
6. A
7. S
8. A

Exercise 7 (p. 160)
Answers will vary.

Exercise 8 (p. 161)
1. b
2. a
3. c
4. a
5. b
6. c
7. a
8. b
9. b

Exercise 9 (p. 162)
1. a
2. c
3. a
4. c
5. b

Exercise 10 (p. 163)
 a. to take a lesser or lower position; to become secondary to someone or something
 b. to feel very comfortable in a place, like it was your own home
 c. to take a scheduled train, bus, plane, and so on
 d. to return to an earlier period or time

Exercise 11 (p. 164)
 1. William Marshall, his father, told Thurgood from an early age to treat everyone with <u>respect</u> but never to let any <u>insult</u> go by without standing up for himself.
 2. As part of the protective blanket she wrapped around <u>Thurgood,</u> Grandma Mary also gave him practical <u>advice</u> about his <u>chances</u> as a young black man in turn-of-the century <u>America.</u> "Your mother and father want you to be a dentist or a doctor, something like that," she told him. "And I <u>hope</u> you make it. But just in case you don't, I'm going to teach you how to <u>cook.</u> And you know why? You've never seen an <u>unemployed</u> black cook."
 3. Colored High and Training School was Baltimore's first high school for <u>blacks.</u> The school had no <u>library,</u> no <u>cafeteria,</u> and no <u>gym</u> when Thurgood arrived. "The school's in urgent need <u>of equipment.</u> It is sadly short of anything like an adequate <u>supply,</u>" the principal had written in his <u>annual</u> report to the superintendent of public instruction.
 4. At age sixteen, Thurgood <u>Marshall</u> began to change. The teasing, often goofy boy began a <u>journey</u> of experiences that opened his eyes to the painful <u>realities</u> of economic and <u>racial</u> problems crippling most black Americans.
 5. Marshall returned from his trips to the Deep <u>South</u> more <u>convinced</u>

than ever of the need to <u>overthrow</u> the <u>racial</u> laws that kept southern blacks poor and <u>uneducated.</u>

Exercise 12 (p. 165)
 Answers will vary.

Exercise 13 (p. 165)
 1. Thirteenth
 2. Nineteenth
 3. Twenty-first
 4. Seventeenth
 5. Fifteenth
 6. Eighteenth

Exercise 14 (p. 167)
 Answers will vary.

Unit 9: Frank Lloyd Wright

Vocabulary Preview

 Preview 1 (p. 169)
 1. interlocking
 2. oscillate
 3. subside
 4. reinforce
 5. adjacent

 Preview 2 (p. 169)
 1. b
 2. d
 3. a
 4. e
 5. c

Reading Preview (p. 170)
 1. b
 2. a
 3. b

Comprehension Check (p. 177)
 1. F
 2. T
 3. F
 4. F
 5. F
 6. F
 7. T
 8. T

Critical Thinking (p. 178)

Answers will vary.

Exercise 1 (p. 179)
1. sub, subculture
2. super, superego
3. sub, subdivided
4. sub, subheadings
5. super, superpower
6. sub, submarine
7. super, superimposed
8. sub, subordinate

Exercise 2 (p. 180)
1. fragmentary
   Meaning: incomplete; broken into pieces
2. military
   Meaning: relating to soldiers, arms, or war
3. rudimentary
   Meaning: crude; primitive
4. stationary
   Meaning: still; unmoving
5. summary
   Meaning: comprehensive; covering the main points
6. voluntary
   Meaning: done by one's own choice or free will

Exercise 3 (p. 181)
1. e
2. g
3. a
4. f
5. b
6. c
7. h
8. d
Additional synonyms will vary.

Exercise 4 (p. 181)
1. mobile
2. require
3. liberal
4. modify
5. inferior
6. texture

Exercise 5 (p. 182)
Set A
1. b
2. e
3. d
4. a

Set B
5. h
6. i
7. f
8. j

Set C
9. m
10. k
11. o
12. l

Exercise 6 (p. 183)
1. fragments
2. military
3. rudiments
4. stationary
5. summarize
6. voluntary

Exercise 7 (p. 183)
1. chief
2. confront
3. subsidence, subsiding
4. crisis
5. reverse
6. style
7. client
8. magnitude

Exercise 8 (p. 184)
1. c
2. b
3. c
4. b
5. a

Exercise 9 (p. 185)
Answers will vary.

Exercise 10 (p. 186)
Text 1
1. The people living there were wealthy; they had plenty of money.

2. unusual, Wright never collaborated with anyone
3. take its inspiration from (Mount Sinai). He may have chosen it for its meaning and significance in Jewish history.
4. unite the dynamic spirit, ancient spirit, the only man who could design the temple
5. being the cradle of the United States' democratic way of life

Text 2
1. Tabernacle means *tent*. The temple was shaped like a tent or a mountain.
2. Steel and concrete supports. There were three supports.
3. The shape was hexagonal. A hexagon has six sides.
4. The tripod rested on a concrete base. Three "wings" came up from the base.
5. The inside of the auditorium is shaped like a shallow dish sitting under a pyramid.

Exercise 11 (p. 189)
   Answers will vary.

Exercise 12 (p. 190)
   Answers will vary.

Exercise 13 (p. 190)
   Answers will vary.

Review Unit 3

I. (p. 191)
   Set A: 4, 2, 3
   Set B: 2, 1, 4
   Set C: 4, 5, 3

II. (p. 191)
   1. S
   2. A
   3. S
   4. S
   5. A
   6. S
   7. A
   8. A

III. (p. 192)
   1. i
   2. f
   3. g
   4. b
   5. a
   6. j
   7. c
   8. e

IV. (p. 192)
   1. peso
   2. lira
   3. deutsche mark
   4. pound
   5. franc
   6. peso

V. (p. 192)
   1. village
   2. sun-dried brick
   3. peppers
   4. River
   5. peppers
   6. River

VI. (p. 193)
   1. constructs
   2. focus
   3. motives
   4. texture
   5. lenses
   6. attached

How to Make Your Own Vocabulary Word Index Cards and Vocabulary Notebook

1. Write the following words on cards, approximately business card size.
2. On the back of each card write the meaning or meanings of the word in your native language. If it's helpful to you, write the phonetic pronunciation of the word and a sample sentence containing the word.
3. Practice with these cards when you have time. Look at the word on the front. Try to remember the meaning of the word. Check the back of the card to see if you are correct. Retest yourself on the cards you miss.
4. Review the vocabulary cards periodically. This will help you remember and master these words.
5. In addition to making vocabulary word index cards, you may want to make your own vocabulary notebook. If you read or hear a word you do not know, consult your dictionary for the meaning of the word. Write this in a vocabulary notebook. If it's helpful to you, write the phonetic pronunciation of the word and a sample sentence containing the word. By the time you finish the notebook, you will have your own academic learner dictionary.

absorb
academic (academically)
accumulate
accurate (accuracy)
adjacent
affluence (affluent)
align
alternative
anthropology
approximate (approximately)
aspect
asset

assure
atmosphere
attach
attribute
authorize (authorities)
benefit
bureaucracy (bureaucratic)
capacity
carbon (carbonize)
catalog
cell
circulate (circulation)
circumstance

client
comment
compute
conclude
confine
congress (congressional)
conserve (conservatively)
constant (constantly)
constitute (constitution)
construct (construction)
contrary
contribute
convene

credible (credibility)
currency
cylinder
data
deflect
deliberate (deliberately)
democracy (Democrats)
deprive
detriment (detrimental)
deviate (deviation)
diffuse
discern
discrete
distinct (distinction)
distort (distortion)
diverge (divergent)
diverse
doctrine
drain
elaborate
elevate (elevation)
emphasize
energy
episode
estimate
evaporate
eventual (eventually)
exclude (exclusive)
execute (executive)
expose
extract
fluent
focus
found
fragment
frantic
frustrate
fuel
fund
horror
image

impact
imperial
impulse
incline
indigenous
inferior
inherent (inherently)
inhibit
injure (injury)
integrate
intense
interlock
interview
intimacy
intuitive (intuitively)
invade
invest (investor)
investigate (investigation)
journal (journalism)
lens
liberal
linguistic (linguist)
locate
magic
magnitude
maintain
major
manifest
material
mobile
modify
monarch
motive (motivate)
myth (mythical)
negative
obvious (obviously)
occur
oscillate
oxygen
perspective
physical (physically)

pole
policy
positive
precede (precedent)
precise (precision)
previous (previously)
process
prosper (prosperous)
publish
refute
reinforce
release
require
respond (response)
revive
rhythm
role
route
secure
sex
shift
similar
simultaneous (simultane-
ously)
speculate (speculation)
status
stress (stressful)
style (stylized)
subside
survey
symbol (symbolic)
technique
tense (tension)
texture
tradition (traditional)
ultimate (ultimately)
utilize (utilities)
verify
vertical (vertically)
violate (violation)